The Voyages of the
Clontarf

by Marolyn Diver

Ancestral Journeys
of New Zealand
Series

Many thanks to the kind descendants of the *Clontarf* passengers for their excellent contributions to this book. By doing so they have helped to ensure their relatives are more then just an obscure name on a passenger list.

An extra big thank you to the following people for their help, feedback and expertise.

David Dudfield

Anna Purgar & Latisha Dowling

Karyn Wilson (Rouse family 1859-60)

Barbara Snook (Sadler/Barton Families 1859-60)

Lindsay Butterfield (Butterfield Family 1859-60)

Carole Smith (McLauchlan and Galletly Family 1859 -60)

Don Gregg (Newsome Family 1858-59)

Wayne P Marriott (Brake Family 1858-59)

Aaron May (Ashton Family 1858-59)

Allan Harkess (Harkess Family 1858-59)

Belinda Lansley (Lord Family 1859-60)

Margaret Lyne (Waller Family 1859-60)

Dornie Publishing Company

Grasmere, Invercargill

www.dorniepublishing.tk

Original text © Marolyn Diver 2013

Images © named individuals, institutions.

All rights reserved.

ISBN 978-0-473-18466-7

Cover design by Strawberrymouse Designs

Dedicated to all those who travelled so very far, and who inadvertently

gave the generations to come a much better chance at life.

Thank you.

Marolyn Diver

(Great-Great-Granddaughter of Eliza Coatman, *Clontarf* passenger 1859-60)

CONTENTS

Introduction

1.	The Ship	----------------------------------	9
2.	First Voyage	----------------------------------	25
3.	Passengers	----------------------------------	35
4.	Second Voyage	----------------------------------	43
5.	Passengers	----------------------------------	63
6.	Passenger Lists	----------------------------------	71

Bibliography

Introduction

This book is an attempt to uncover the history of one of New Zealand's lesser known emigrant ships and to share this research with a wider audience of NZ history enthusiasts and genealogists searching for their ancestors on the ship.

In the course of putting this publication together a number of questions and issues arose about the reliability of some information sources. The research process was at times confused by inaccurate newspaper reports, incomplete shipping logs, and the personal biases of the shipboard diaries. One might imagine how a half-deaf shipping clerk, tipsy ship-master, or bored typesetter could have, and often did, affect our perceptions of history through their simple mistakes!

While researching I found many of the names on the shipping lists were either spelt wrong or not even present. By the end of the process I had worked through and assessed four complete shipping lists and combined the information into a master-list, which I trust is the most accurate one to date. By scouring the shipboard diaries I also found several more deaths on the ill fated 1859-60 voyage than were ever mentioned in official sources. Even then some diaries implied additional fatalities; yet without any corroborating evidence I could not include them. Finally, I managed to uncover the mystery of what became of the *Clontarf* after her two voyages to New Zealand. Some believed she disappeared on the return journey to England, with all hands perishing with her.

Ultimately, once the sources were compared and evaluated, and the narrative was firmly established; all these tentative clues became useful parts in piecing together what I hope is a balanced historical perspective of the *Clontarf*.

In essence, *The Voyages of the Clontarf* is a forgotten story of tragedy at sea, overlooked heroes, valiant sacrifices, and finding hope in the promise of a new land.

Note

Sadly, for so many more reasons than just writing this book, during my research the devastating Christchurch earthquake of the 22nd February 2011 occurred. I was in the midst of requesting two further diaries from Lyttelton Museum which were to complete the account of the first voyage (1858-60). Because of the destruction I decided to continue with the publication without them and this is why the first voyage may seem a little less explored compared with the second. I hope that in the future I can extend on this but for now, my friends and family in Canterbury, and the people of Lyttleton, Christchurch, and the surrounding areas have a long road to recovery ahead of them. Our thoughts are with you all.

Marolyn. (March 2011)

The Ship

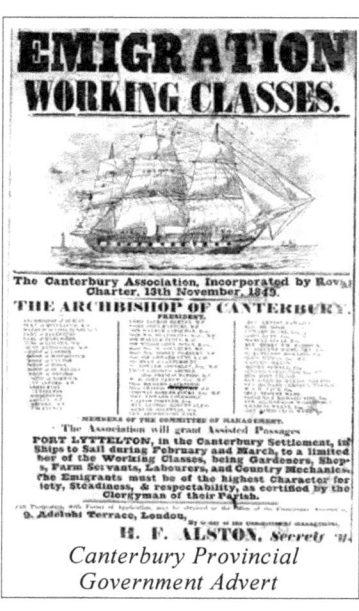

Canterbury Provincial Government Advert

English built ship "La Hogue." Built 1855. Similar, make, tonnage and date to Clontarf.

The *Clontarf* was a full poop deck, frigate-built, packet ship constructed in 1852 by H. N. Jones of Quebec, Canada, for the shipping company Willis, Gann & Co. of England. This shipping company was one of a handful of dedicated emigrant ship-masters commissioned by the Canterbury Provincial Government to assist emigration to New Zealand from 1853 until 1862. Along with the *Clontarf*, Willis, Gann & Co. also owned and operated around 16 other ships including the: *Zealandia, Maori, Cresswell* and *Cashmere*. All of which had lucrative careers long after Willis, Gann & Co. bowed out of the shipping business in 1862.

The term "frigate-built" entailed that she had a raised quarter-deck and forecastle, with imitation black gun ports and a white band painted down each side of the hull. This naval style was utilized as a ploy to frighten off pirates; a common practice for ships operating in distant waters. This ferocious warship-like appearance was a good selling point for the companies marketing safe voyages in dangerous sea. A "packet" ship was originally a vessel employed to carry mail packets to and from British colonies and outposts, typically departed on a regular schedule. The "packet" designation remained in use even as the ships upgraded to accommodate for more passengers than postal deliveries.

However for all these terms *Clontarf* was technically a "clipper." Clipper ships were built comparatively long and narrow with three or more masts, a large sail area, a square rig and were considered one of the fastest sailing ships of the 19th century.

For the first five years of her life *Clontarf* ferried migrants and freight from Europe to the outer regions of Asia, Pacific, and the Americas. On some voyages she was patronised solely by a wealthy dignitary and his entourage of servants; whilst on others, her hull was the temporary abode of assorted riff-raff who were delivered at *Her Majesty's Pleasure* to the penitentiary at Port Arthur, Australia. She also couriered spices, supplies and exotic creatures to and from the major ports in the West Indies, South America, and Africa. However with all her worldly adventures, it was at this time she had her first brush with tragedy. On August 16th 1856, while under Captain John Allen, *Clontarf* collided with the French Brig *Henriette* off the port of Blyth, Northumberland, sinking the brig in minutes and killing eight members of the French crew. It was assumed the French vessel was at fault as *Clontarf* was all but stationary at the time of the collision. Mercifully *Clontarf* recovered somewhat unscathed from the incident, both structurally and legally.

By time the Canterbury Provincial Government commissioned Willis, Gann & Co. to bring emigrants to New Zealand, *Clontarf* was still in it's adolescence but had seen the world tenfold. The Canterbury Association had first established an assisted emigration scheme in 1848 to bring young, fit, skilled workers to the South Island. This scheme was later adopted by the provincial government after the Association was dissolved c.1853. Each assisted passenger's fare on the voyage was adjusted according to their trade (labourers and farm hands were highly sought after to develop the new farms on the Canterbury Plains). For this discount the immigrants were then obliged to work off the balance once they reached their destination and also to remain in the region for an allocated amount of time. The opportunity outweighed the hardship and the debt was often repaid within a year, leaving them financially unencumbered to prosper in the new land.

Commanders

Clontarf's main skipper was a Captain John T. Allen who commanded her on numerous voyages after construction (1852) then onwards to her first voyage to New Zealand (1858) and beyond. It was advertised that he was to command her second voyage to New Zealand in 1859; however for reasons unknown, he was replaced by part-owner Captain A.W. Barclay Esq. Superstitious sailors might suggest that the ship was unhappy with Allen's replacement for uncharacteristically her luck seemed to change.

By all accounts Capt. Barclay was an upstanding man of character with untold years of sailing expertise behind him; he had once before captained *Clontarf* to Australia in 1853. Yet none of his experience could prepare him for this voyage. Barclay was physically and mentally pushed to the brink through personal illness, bad luck and an unfortunately high passenger death toll. It would be fair to say he arrived in New Zealand a changed man. After he returned the ship to England one might assume he wanted to wash his hands of *Clontarf*; but advertisements for later voyages up until 1862 indicate that he was still employed as her captain. However this could have been an oversight on pre-paid adverts, uncorrected in the New Zealand newspapers; or perhaps he signed a contract to be at the helm for three years. In any case *Clontarf* undertook few, if any, voyages in that time. Following Barclay's stint, Capt. Allen was recorded back at the helm of his ship which would, for but a short time, loyally abide his commands once more.

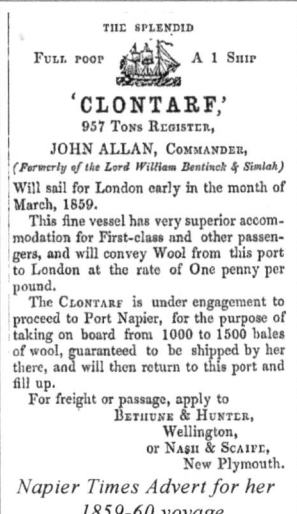

Napier Times Advert for her 1859-60 voyage

Crew

A typical crew of a clipper ship

By law all emigrants crossing the seas from England to New Zealand had to have their names and occupations written into the ship's log. These were officially recorded again at their port of arrival, however this was not always the case for the crew. Quite often sailors unofficially emigrated; they worked for their passage but remained unrecorded in the logbooks.

The standard crew for a voyage without migrants on the *Clontarf* consisted of the Captain, First Mate or Officer, Second Mate, a midshipman (apprentice officer), ship's carpenter, boatswain, 9-10 able and ordinary seamen, and the "boy" or cabin boy, used for mundane low level duties. With emigrants to accommodate, *Clontarf's* crew doubled to at least 40. Amongst the new crew were the ship's Doctor and Constable, both essential for the welfare of the passengers. For the wealthy Chief Cabin passengers there were stewards; some who were tasked to provide around the clock service for those that paid for the privilege. Other important additions to the crew were the Ship's Cook and Passenger's Cook. The main difference being that the Passenger's Cook made basic food for the masses; the Ship's Cook catered for the refined tastes of the Chief Cabin, Second Cabin and the crew. With woman and children aboard there was the need for a matron to keep the single woman apart from the single men, and also for a teacher to keep the children learning and out of the crew's way. On occasion there was a priest or minister present on the voyage.

The average crewman could earn around £7 (NZ$950) a month for the journey and were well fed with very comfortable accommodation. However the bulk of the wage was in the return voyage which could be as high as £100 each. This was paid as an incentive for loyalty and commitment to the voyage. But the hellish pace set by some captains meant that mutinies and port desertions were not uncommon.

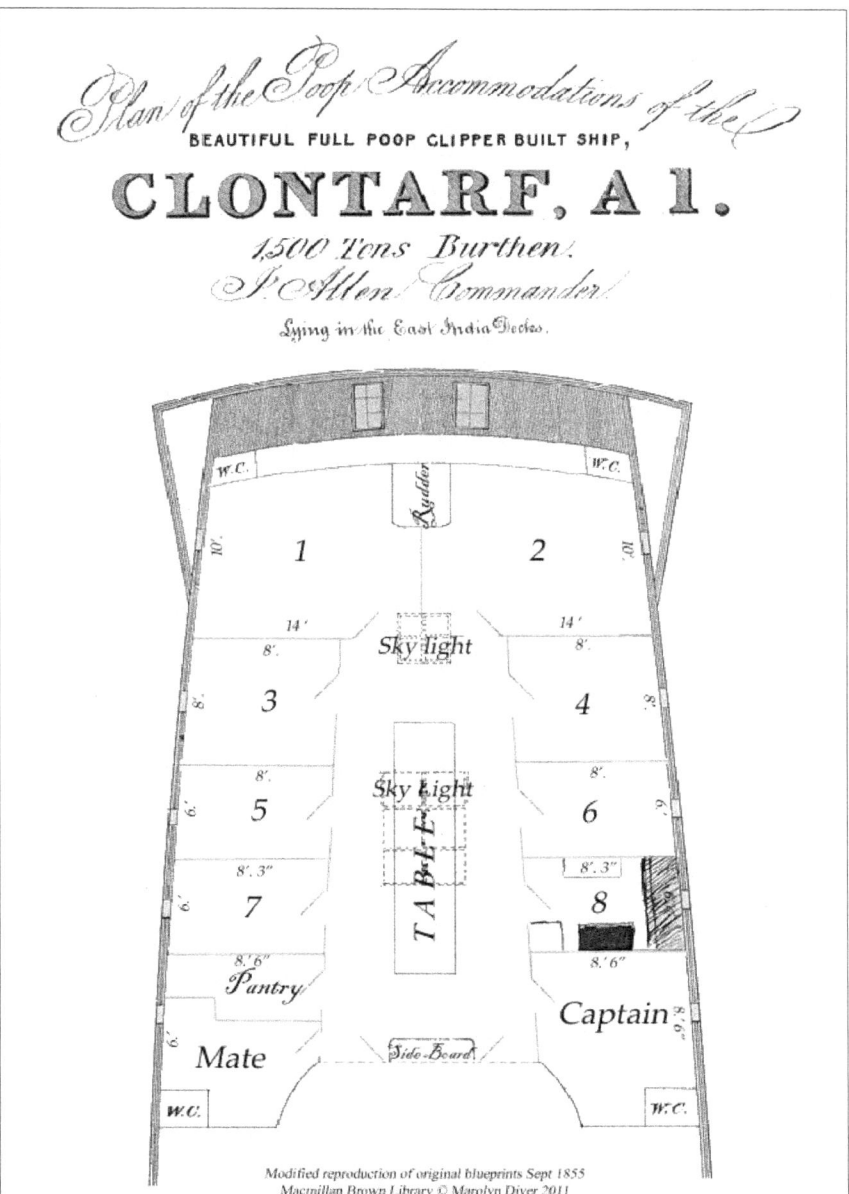

Accommodation

- **A.** Chief Cabin, measuring 6 ft by 7ft.

Price if occupied by one person £60 (NZ$5500 today*). If occupied by two $40 each. (NZ$3500)

- **B.** *Second Cabin*, measuring 6ft 9in by 7 ft 6in.

For 4 people or a family, price £25 per adult (NZ$2200)

- **C.** *Second Cabin*, measuring 3ft 6in by 7ft 8in. For married couples.

For Steerage and Assisted Immigrant Accommodation

- **D.** *Steerage*. Enclosed cabin measuring 7 to 8 ft square. For 6 people at £20 each. (NZ$1700)

- **E.** *Steerage. Enclosed* cabin measuring 3ft 4in by 8ft for married couples.

- **F.** *Steerage.* Open berths at £18 each. (NZ$1500)

- **T.** Dining tables and seating area.

Rates of Assisted Immigrant passage:

Married agricultural labourer and wife, under 40yrs	£10 (NZ$961.70)
-Children Under 14	£2 (NZ$240.40)
-Infants Free	
Married merchant and wife	£16 (NZ$1442.50)
-Children each	£4 (NZ$360.60)
-Infants Free	
Single Merchant	£10 (NZ$961.70)
Single agricultural labourer	£8 (NZ$721.30)

* Currency conversion is from the pound value 161 years ago in the 2011 currency market. It is then converted into New Zealand dollars.

The Ship

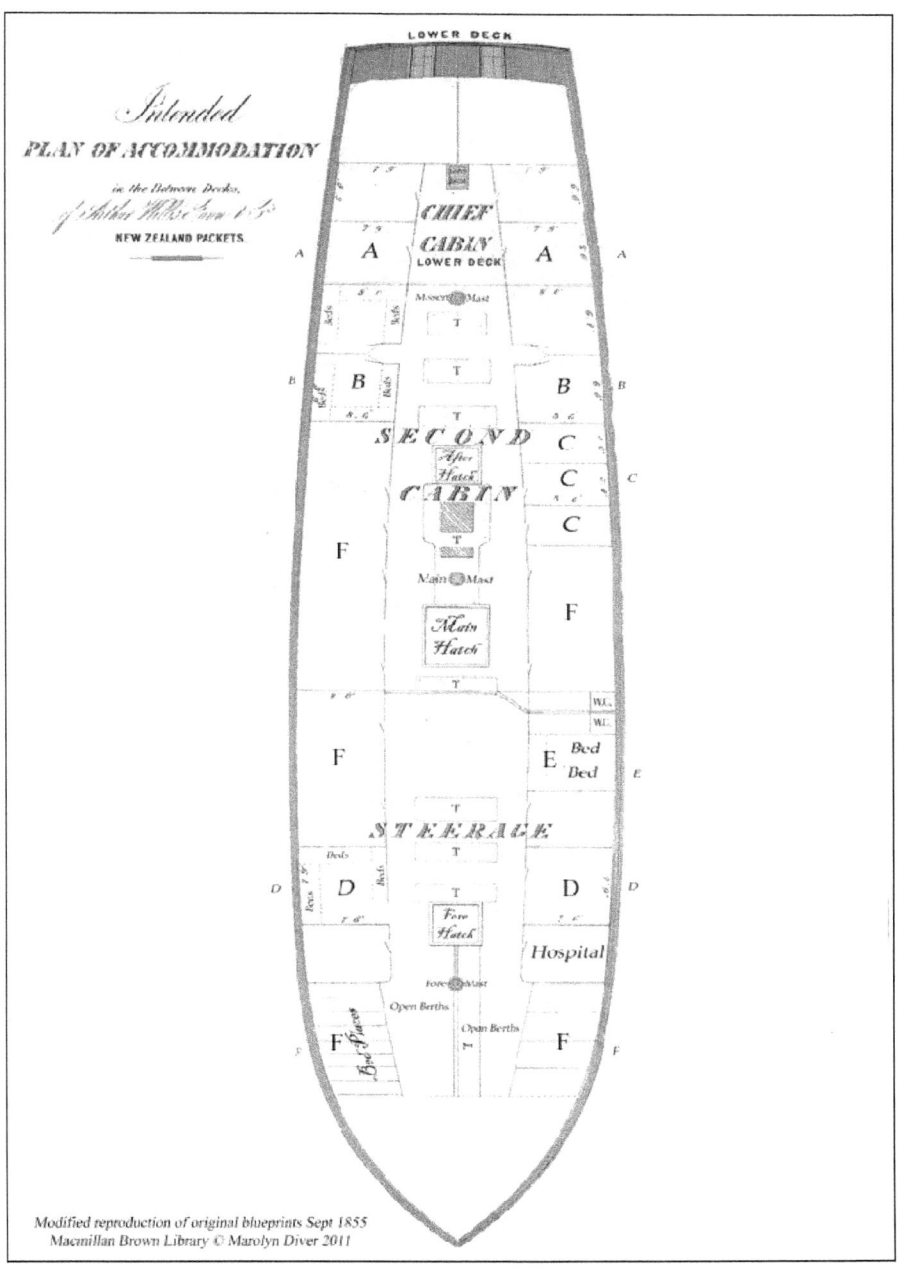

The St. Vincent living quarters below deck. "London News" Illustration 1844.

Life On

Passengers of the Chief Cabin provided their own furniture, beds, and other home comforts they might like inside their comparatively spacious private cabins. The ship supplied a table, cutlery, linen, glasses, plates and if required, a personal attendant. Second Cabin had shared rooms with six bunked berths per room and only part-time attendants for cleaning. Steerage and assisted emigrants had open berths that were segregated into single male and females quarters; the later was chaperoned by a matron at a respectable distance from the males. Families were massed together at the front of the ship in what must have looked like a combination of an out-of-control daycare, rowdy pub and knitting circle. Most of the passengers, including Second Cabin, were required to supply their own bedding, utensils, cups, plates, even their own teapots. Twice a day the cook prepared a meal for them but at other times they had to fend for themselves.

Water Closet/Toilets (noted on the blueprints as W.C.) were located at each corner on the Chief Cabin and crew decks. Second Cabin passengers were permitted to use these facilities, however the poor steerage passengers had to make do with one of only two toilets in their section. Time and biological requirements meant that using an open porthole as their own private en-suite was not entirely unheard of and by no means beneath those travelling in such cramped and uncomfortable conditions.

Meals

Food was allocated according to the passenger's cabin status and was rationed out strictly. Even water was given less to steerage and the emigration class. Interestingly, lime juice seems to have been made available to them and not the chief passengers. The vitamins in the juice were considered more beneficial than water alone.

On board was a large chicken coup which provided plenty of fresh eggs, a pig pen for fresh meat, and passengers often had cows, sheep and other farm animals in the hold which ensured a ready supply of goods to barter with.

Personal supplies of liquor were forbidden on the ship, however alcohol was offered for purchase by the ship stewards. This was to maintain a tight hold on alcohol consumption *"for the better preservation of order on the ship."*

Passengers paid four shillings (NZ$19) for a bottle of port or wine *"of the finest quality"*. While beer was around NZ$5. Spirits were only permitted to be sold to the chief passengers. In most instances only a select few members of the crew had access to the alcohol supply, for obvious reasons.

WEEKLY DIETARY SCALE FOR EACH ADULT PASSENGER.

Articles.	Chief Cabin.	Second Cabin.	Steerage.
Preserved Meats	1½ lb.	1½ lb.	1 lb.
Preserved Salmon	½ "	—	—
Assorted Soups	1 "	—	—
Soup and Bouilli	—	⅓ lb.	—
York Ham	1 "	½ "	—
Tripe	½ "	—	—
Fish	½ "	¼ lb.	—
Prime India Beef	½ "	1 "	1¼ lb.
Irish Mess Pork	1 "	1½ "	1 "
Biscuit	3 "	4¼ "	3½ "
Flour	4¼ "	4¼ "	3 "
Rice	1 "	1 "	½ "
Barley	¼ "	½ "	—
Peas	½ pint	½ pint	½ pint
Oatmeal	½ "	½ "	1 "
Preserved Milk	½ "	—	—
Sugar, refined	½ lb.	—	—
Sugar, raw	¼ "	1 lb.	1 lb.
Lime Juice	—	6 oz.	6 oz.
Tea	3 oz.	1½ oz.	1½ oz.
Coffee	5 "	3 "	2 "
Butter	½ lb.	½ lb.	6 "
Cheese	½ "	¼ "	—
Currants	¼ "	¼ "	—
Raisins, Valentia	½ "	½ "	½ lb.
Raisins, Muscatel	¼ "	—	—
Suet	½ "	6 oz.	6 oz.
Preserved Carrots	½ "	—	—
Pickles	¼ pint	¼ pint	¼ pint
Vinegar	¼ "	—	—
Mustard	½ oz.	½ oz.	½ oz.
Pepper	½ "	¼ "	¼ "
Salt	2 "	2 "	2 "
Potatoes, fresh or	3½ lb.	3½ lb.	2 lb.
Preserved ditto	½ "	½ "	½ "
Water	28 quarts	21 quarts	21 quarts

Taken from the Wills, Gann & Co regulations documentation 1857

Dancing Between the Decks

<u>Shows</u>: Quite often passengers were encouraged to stage their own shows. Some entertained by showing off their musical abilities. Others read aloud from books. Budding actors would re-enact classical plays which were always cheered on with unbridled enthusiasm, even if little actual talent existed amongst them.

<u>Dances</u>: Any passengers that showed an inkling of musical talent were strongly encouraged to sing and play at the regular social dance occasions. These spontaneously arose as a fun diversion to fill in the dark dreary nights.

<u>Lectures</u>: Whilst not strictly classed as entertainment, certain members of the passengers and crew who had been to New Zealand before would hold lectures for the passengers to prepare them for the new land.

Sightseeing was a large part of entertainment

<u>Wonders of the Natural World</u>: The voyage itself was a scientific wonderland: mysterious creatures from the deep, fascinating new bird species, exotic lands in the distance, and the ever changing constellations of the night sky found a ready audience in both the passengers and crew.

Misfortune

Forces of Nature

As with any voyage, Mother Nature could be a ship's best friend or worst enemy. On some voyages the sun would smile down on them as the trade winds whisked them to their destination at mighty speeds. On other voyages the winds might fail, the oceans could swell tremendously, and rain could pour relentlessly for the entire trip. Of all these voyaging scenarios the biggest fear for both the passengers and crew was a sinking ship. Nevertheless most vessels of this type were surprisingly resilient. Records show that some of the emigrant ships that sustained substantial damage could limp along the entire voyage. They could take water, spring leaks, lose sails and masts, but be repaired and on their way the very next day. The pause for repairs would cause a slight inconvenience to the passengers but since this was long before the era of suing for 'emotional damage and distress', people took delays as given and got on with their lives. *Clontarf* saw her fair share of nature's vengeance; not only from the weather, but also from the misfortunes of disease, death and plain bad luck.

Illness

During the 1859-60 voyage *Clontarf* suffered the highest death rate from illness of any emigrant ship to New Zealand in the 19th century. On a normal emigration voyage it might be expected that around five people would die from frailty, accidents and births at sea. *Clontarf* suffered 41 deaths. Measles and whooping cough spread quickly amongst the children in the ship; typhoid, diphtheria and alcohol poisoning impacted on the adults. Tropical disease was also suspected, possibly resulting from a large squall hitting the ship and filling the lower decks with water just as they reached the tropical belt. The hot, humid, stagnant conditions may have been a breeding ground for disease and by the time they reached the cool sub-Antarctic climate it would have been too late. Various illnesses had taken a toll on the children and left many of the adults bed ridden. The "plague" did not leave the *Clontarf* until the ship reached the outer waters of New Zealand.

The Sinking of the Birkenhead Clipper Ship – Charles Dixon

<u>Gone Before Her Time</u>

Clontarf operated for just three more years after her New Zealand voyages. Her reputation as a "doomed ship" preceded her and she was eventually stood down by the Canterbury Provincial Government as advertisements for her passage to New Zealand had few takers. Instead, she returned again to her old duties of ferrying cargo and full-fare passengers across the Indian, Atlantic and Pacific oceans. By this time Willis, Gann and Co. had dissolved their shipping business, and *Clontarf* was possibly operating under the flag of Shaw, Savill and Co.

On the 13th of January 1863 on route from Queenstown, County Cork, Ireland to Pensacola, Florida, USA with just one passenger and 20 crew, the Clontarf encountered heavy weather and was battered so violently that she began to leak. Sadly her resistance against the harsh seas had come to an end. The Captain, seeing that the she was sinking fast made a desperate distress signal which was answered by the ship *Progress*. The crew of the *Clontarf* quickly escaped into the lifeboats, one boat manned by the valiant captain of *Progress* himself who battled the violent swell to safely rescue all who had been on board. There they watched into the fading light as *Clontarf* sang her swan song and succumbed at last to the relentless ocean. Thus came the end of the ship *Clontarf*. Her spirit put to rest in the deep dark waters of the North Atlantic Ocean.

Captain A. Jolly of the Progress and his crew were later awarded for their assistance and bravery that day.

Notes

The Ship

Voyage One

Sept 16ᵗʰ 1858 – Jan 5thᵗʰ 1859

A. WILLIS, GANN, & CO.'S
PACKETS
BETWEEN
LONDON AND NEW ZEALAND.

The following first-class Ships (with others) are intended to be despatched to both Southern and Northern Ports, as regular traders, viz.:—

NAME OF MASTER	COMMANDER	TONS
Joseph Fletcher	J. Pook	1,100
Chapman	R. Harland	1,200
Maori	G. Petherbridge	1,000
Myrtle	J. G. Mordue	1,000
Mariner	C. E. Fraser	1,000
Cashmere	G. Pearson	1,000
Egmont	S. C. Gibson	1,100
Cresswell	W. C. Barnett	800
Sir Edward Paget	T. Wycherley	900
Euphemus	J. Howard	1,000
John Masterman	John M'Buvie	1,060
Clontarf	T. Allen	1,500
Caduceus	G. Cass	1,500
Zealandia	J. Foster	1,200
Harwood (new)		800
Strathallan	J. Smith	800
Simlah		800

The undersigned, agents for the above line of vessels, are authorised to arrange with settlers at Nelson and New Plymouth who may be desirous of bringing their friends in Great Britain out to this colony, and are prepared either to pay the passage money at once to them, or give satisfactory security for its payment on the arrival of the vessel.

Further particulars on application to

NASH & SCAIFE,
Nelson and New Plymouth.

Napier Times Advertisement, 1858

Donati's Comet. Companion to the Clontarf up until early November.

Clontarf set sail from Gravesend on 16th of September 1858 with 470 souls on board and fair weather to guide them gently on their way. The world was abuzz at this time due to the presence of the spectacular Donati's Comet. The comet's tail swept majestically across the night sky, providing inspiration and contemplation for famous artists, world leaders and scientists alike. It seems that the passengers never tired of admiring the comet's wonders over the passing nights and the diaries all record a collective sigh as they gradually lost sight of her in the night sky in late October - early November. But still, for now, it shone above them brightly like a comforting beacon as they sailed through the Bay of Biscay and out into the open waters of the Atlantic in search of the dependable trade winds.

On the 3rd of October just after *Clontarf* sighted Porto Santo (a small group of islands north-east of Madeira) diary entries record the appearance of a mysterious man who had been kept separate from the other passengers and only brought above decks 18 days into the voyage. Court documents would later prove that this gentlemen was in fact a stow-away who had been caught eight days beforehand and was kept in the brig until the resident constable had decided what to do with him. This truth, unfortunately, was far removed from the passengers speculations that he may have been a rich Baron travelling incognito; or a Prince from a foreign land. It was perhaps a good thing that the passengers had such wild imaginations, as he remained un-manacled amongst them for the remainder of the passage and stuck up a rapport with the ship's crew who allowed him to work off some of his passage. He was eventually brought in front of the magistrate at Lyttelton and told to pay the remainder of his fare within the year, officially grounding him in New Zealand.

Voyage One

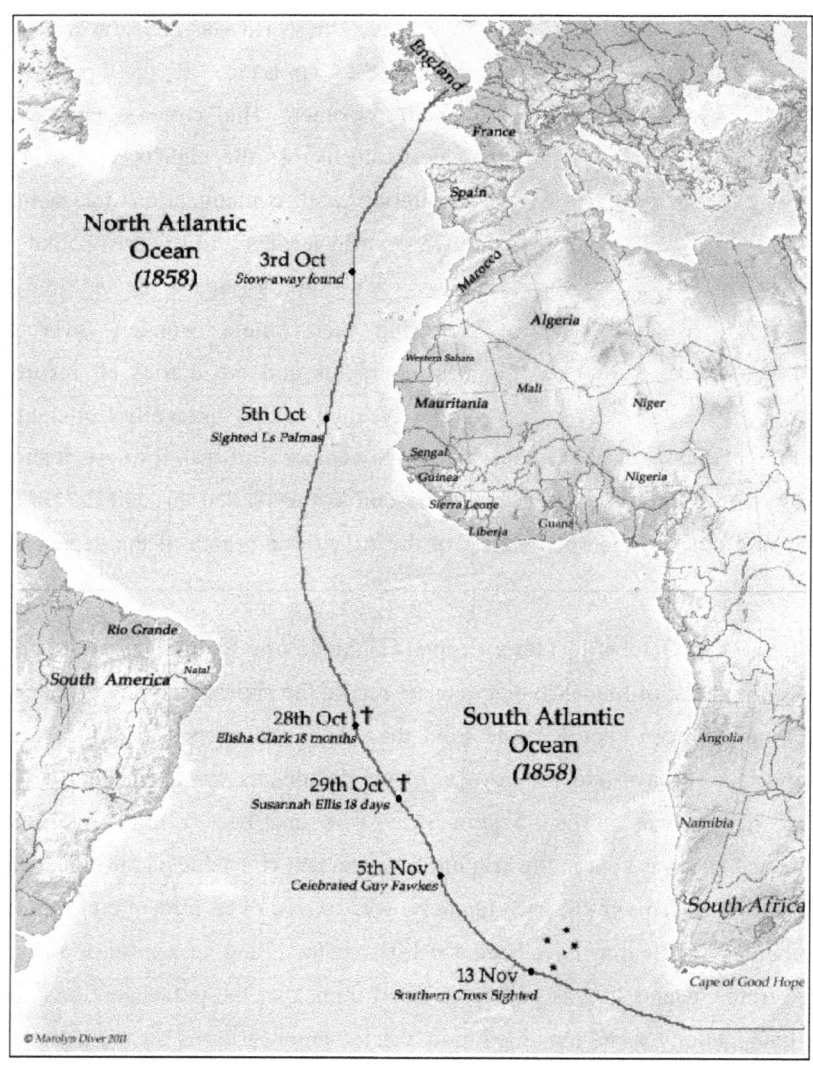

Boxing was a popular form of entertainment on the voyage

One of the amusements of the ship, a popular one for the men, was to participate in and boisterously encourage boxing matches.

A champion had reigned for some weeks on the ship until one evening his wife, who had forbidden him to continue, found him in the midst of winning another match. She angrily boxed her husband's ears and dragged him below deck. He did not dare show his face in the ring again. All that fought afterwards felt that without the champion there was no standard to reach so the men resolved to drink and play cards for the rest of the voyage.

On the 5th of November the passengers celebrated the anniversary of Guy Fawkes on-board. A small controlled bonfire was constructed and effigies were burned. Drinks were served and a warm-hearted celebration continued well into the night.

With the winds fine, and her speed a swift 12 knots on some days, it was not long before the passengers were to lay eyes on the night sky that would soon be theirs forever. The Southern Cross came in to view on the 13th of November and now that Donati's Comet had abandoned them they once more took comfort looking up into the night. It served as a beacon of anticipation of things to come. Land was close and although the journey had been fair, all were wary of the ocean and longed to feel dry land once more.

Southern Cross marked in the night sky

Voyage One

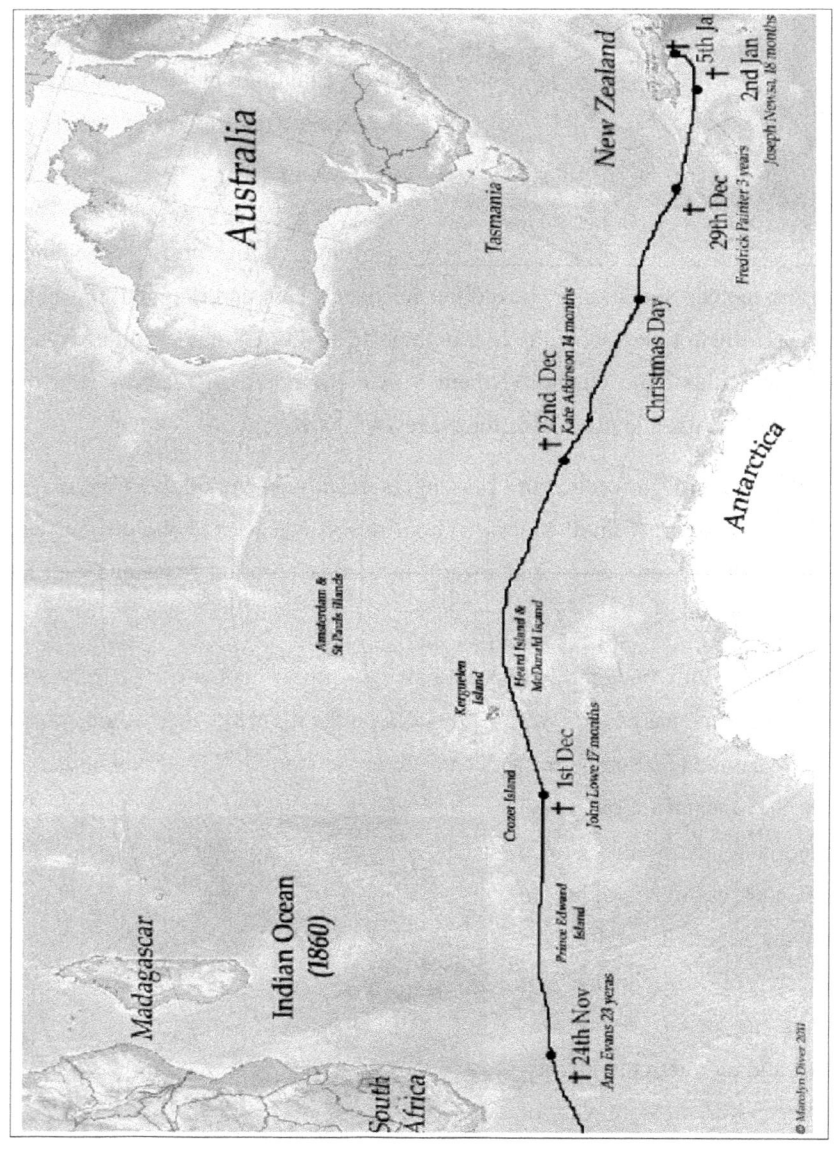

Lyttelton Port. From the Illustrated London News 1863

On 7th December the passengers drew a lottery to see who would be the closest to guessing when they would see New Zealand. This was apparently something of a tradition for Capt. Allen and his crew as he put up a part-refund of passage as a prize for the winner. Some of the Chief passengers admirably chose seemingly impossible dates for the lottery in order to have the prize go to someone more in need. In any case it was a one of the Chief passengers, a man named Burnell, that won. On the 31st of December, Stewart Island came in to view.

Perhaps in fitting with the ease of this voyage, the only horrific tragedy to befall them occurred once the ship had arrived into Lyttelton Port on the 5th of January. A three year old girl, Mary Charlotte Brake, was scalded to death on the ship. Though because they were in port it was not counted as a ship fatality.

> **RESIDENT MAGISTRATE'S COURT,**
> LYTTELTON.
> FRIDAY, JAN. 7, 1859.
> (Before J. W. HAMILTON, ESQ., R. M.)
> IMMIGRATION AGENT v. GEORGE PHILLIPS.
> Phillips was a stow-away in the ship Clontarf, having concealed himself for the purpose of obtaining a passage out. The prisoner, who stated that he was a cooper by trade and had worked his passage out, requested Captain Allan to allow him to work home again. To this the master, who gave prisoner a good character, demurred, on the ground of his not being a seaman. It was finally arranged that Phillips should give a promissory note to pay the Provincial Government for his passage, and that he should be allowed 12 months to repay; unless any intention of his leaving the Colony should be manifested. A penalty of 24 hours imprisonment with hard labour was inflicted.

Stow-away George Phillips' court appearance

Deaths and Births
The Clontarf

Deaths
1858
28th October:	Elisha George Clark, 18 months old.
29th October:	Susannah Ellis, aged 18 days old
24h November:	Ann Evans, aged 23 years old
1st December:	John Lowe, 17 months old.
22nd December:	Kate Atkinson, 14 months old.
29th December:	Frederick William Painter, 3 years old.

1859
2nd January:	Joseph Newsome, 18 months old,
5th January:	Mary Charlotte Brake, 3 years old. (died in port)
Unknown Date:	Daughter of Mr & Mrs Turner, stillborn.

9 deaths in total.

Births
Mrs James Pratt – a son
Mrs Joseph Weeber – a daughter
Mrs Joseph Ellis – a daughter
Mrs Charles Turner - a daughter.

Illness
76 counts of illness reported on the ship

Animal Deaths
20 fowls
2 sheep
5 pigs
2 goats
2 dogs

SHIP CLONTARF
FOR WELLINGTON AND PORT NAPIER.

THIS Vessel (weather permitting) will be cleared from this port on THURSDAY NEXT.
All accounts to be rendered to Captain Allan on the previous day.
For freight or passage, apply to
R. LATTER.
Lyttelton, Feb. 1, 1859.

EX CLONTARF.
LEAVING Gravesend on the 10th September, to arrive about the end of this month—
3 cases mixed toys
3 cases haberdashery
Large assortment of mixed muslins, including every kind
A splendid assortment of ribbons to the tune of £300
5 packages saddlery, a small assortment of all kinds
4 packages stationery
A large assortment of hosiery
2 cases sample of Scotch boots
1 case fancy goods and gloves suited to the season
11 cases alpaca, coburg, ginghams, and other stuffs
7 cases white shirts, hoods, ladies' under clothing, &c.
1 case stays, &c.
1 weighing machine, 3 cwt.
IRONMONGERY.
Sickles, reaping hooks, nails of all kinds, hay knives, scythes, pack saddles, spades, shovels, gravel do., lanterns, and every kind of holloware, to the tune of £700; chains, cables, and all kinds of boat gear, to the tune of £40; carpenters' tools of all kinds, gold leaf, paint, and a variety of painters' goods, household tin furniture of every kind, locks and small ironmongery of every description, 25 cases Booth's gin, 60 cases Geneva, best brand, and a large variety of other goods.
JAMES MORRISON & Co.

Clontarf Cargo List - 1858-59

Personal Testimonies

(Lyttelton Times Jan 12th 1859)

THE CLONTARF.

The passengers by this vessel have presented a unanimous testimonial of gratitude and respect to Captain Allan, among whose many voyages the one now finished must, it appears, rank as one of the most agreeable. We are sure that, accustomed as Captain Allan must by this time be to all sorts of expressions of gratitude from large numbers of people, he must be pleased to find his passengers leave him with good humour at the close of a tedious voyage. It will be no less gratification to those who sign the memorial to be able thus to record their satisfaction.

"To Captain Allan;

"We, the undersigned passengers on board the Clontarf from London to New Zealand, beg to congratulate you on the successful termination of our voyage; and with unbounded gratitude to Almighty God for the safe passage of ourselves and families, desire to express to you our heartfelt and sincere thanks for your uniformly kind, considerate, and gentlemanly demeanour throughout the voyage.

"We sincerely hope that by God's blessing you may live many years in the enjoyment of the fruits of your labours, and of social and domestic happiness.

"We also beg through you to thank the officers and crew of the ship for their general kindness and civility.

"We are, sir, yours, &c.

(Signed by names representing 339 persons.)

"On board the Clontarf, Dec. 1858."

The surgeon superintendent of the ship, Dr. Vicary, on his part, received no less than three similar testimonials, one from each of the various sections of the passengers. We publish one of these documents,—that emanating from the 'families,' in the steerage:—

"To George T. Vicary, Esq., Surgeon:

"We, the undersigned, passengers on board the Clontarf from London to New Zealand, beg to convey to you our most sincere thanks for the successful exercise of your professional skill, and for the uniformly kind, attentive, and gentlemanly feeling you have displayed to ourselves and families throughout the voyage.

"We are further desirous of thanking you for your exertions in conducting the religious services on board, and for the care you have manifested for the general moral as well as physical well-being of the passengers.

"That it may please God to bless you with health and prosperity is the sincere wish of, sir,

"Yours faithfully,

(Signed by 91 heads of families, representing 309 souls.)

"On board the ship Clontarf, Dec., 1858."

Passengers 1858–59

Passengers 1858-59

Passengers 1858-59

(In Alphbetical Order)

John Barton Arundel Acland

Acland J. B. A. was born at Rollerton, Devonshire, in 1824. A lawyer by profession, he relinquished this in favour of sheep farming. He first came out to New Zealand in 1854 in the ship *Royal Stuart* with his business partner Charles George Tripp. Together they established Mount Peel Station. He then left Canterbury in March 1857 but returned in January 1859 on the *Clontarf*, writing a shipboard dairy of the voyage. The passengers Chapman and family, along with a single-man, James Rawle, travelled as assisted emigrants but were also in his employment.

Mr and Mrs Mark Beal

Beal, Mark. Mr Beal was born in 1857 at Newcastle-on-Tyne, England. At the age of two years, he accompanied his parents and brother Mark to Lyttelton in *Clontarf*. The family settled at Eyreton after reaching New Zealand, and Mr Beal when on to establish Grange Farm in 1892. He was married in 1889 to Miss Moore and together they had one son and four daughters.

Lucy Brake

Brake, John and Lucy. John was born in Buckland Newton, Dorset, England in 1816 and married Lucy (*nee* Peach) in Sherborne, Dorset. Lucy was born in 1811 in Sherborne. The four children who accompanied them on their voyage were Henry, Harriet, Robert and Mary. Tragically Mary was scalded to death as the ship arrived in Lyttelton. She was buried in Lyttelton Cemetery. John Brake died in 1898 in Christchurch. Lucy died in 1889 at Riccarton, Christchurch. They are buried at St Peter's, Upper Riccarton.

Samuel Cain

Cain, Samuel. Mr Cain was from County Down, Ireland and was born in 1849. He left Ireland for the Colony with his parents in *Clontarf*. Mr Cain was twice married, first to Miss Eagle, who died in 1890, leaving eleven children, and secondly to his first wife's sister, by whom he had three children. He established a farm called "Laurel Grove" in Seadown.

Dulieu, Richard was born in London, and arrived in New Zealand with his family in *Clontarf* in 1859. He was employed for a time by Mr Michael Burke, of Halswell, and was for seven years afterwards a gardener to the late Mr. Guise Brittan. Mr Dulieu began farming on a freehold block of fifty acres at Greenpark, but afterwards increased the area to 300 acres. He died in 1900.

William Gapes

Gapes, William. Born in Saffron Walden 1822, brought up in the cigar making trade in London. He left England in 1858 on the *Clontarf* and worked on various sheep stations including 18 months at A. Cox's Raukapuka Station. In 1871 he took up a farm himself in the valley named by him Gapes Valley. In 1891 he retired to Geraldine. He was a keen amateur painter. His works can still be viewed today and include paintings of the Geraldine district in 1885, Riversley. He died in 1903.

Lilly, George. Mr Lilly was born in Suffolk, England in 1854, and came with his parents to Lyttelton. He was brought up in farming, and started one himself in 1895 on fifty acres of freehold. For nine years Mr Lilly was a member of the Mount Grey Downs school committee, and was a member of the "Rangiora Lodge of Oddfellows." He was married in 1880 to a daughter of Mr. John Vallance, of Mount Grey Downs, and had two sons and two daughters.

John Lister and wife

Lister, John was born in 1833 at Worksop, Nottinghamshire, where he was educated. He came out to the Colony in *Clontarf* in 1859, and settled at Balcairn soon afterwards. Mr Lister took up Crown land and settled on the banks of the Kowai river. He was a churchwarden for many years and taught in the Sunday school, was a member of the school committee, and always ready to help in any good cause or assist a neighbour. He died in July 1897 leaving a widow with three sons and four daughters.

Phillips, George. Stow-away on board the *Clontarf*. A cooper by trade he hid in the ship's cargo hold for 10 days until he was discovered by the ships Constable. He was held in the brig for eight days before it was decided he could join the crew and work off some of his fare. After reaching New Zealand he was charged by law to repay the rest within a year.

Mr James Rowell and wife Elizabeth

Rowell, James and Elizabeth. James was born in Cambridgeshire, England in 1833, and came to New Zealand on the *Clontarf* at the age of 22. He first worked as contractor cutting a drain from the Avon River through Mr Fuche's land, to the English cemetery in Christchurch. He afterwards helped to make the Bridle Path from the Ferry to the Ginger Beer Shop—a name well known in the early days. He married a fellow traveller on the *Clontarf* whose father Mr Philip Martin kept the Black Horse Hotel on Lincoln Road. Mrs Rowell was born in Staffordshire, England in 1836 and they were married during the year of their arrival. Mr and Mrs Rowell had four sons and seven daughters.

Rawle, James came to New Zealand under the employment of Chief passenger John Acland. James' father worked on Aclands father's property in Somersetshire, and there they made each others acquaintances. James Rawle became a shepherd at Mt. Peel, where a hut, yards and gully are named after him.

Edward Sealy

Sealy, Edward Percy was born in England in August, 1839 and was educated at Clifton near Bristol. He arrived at Lyttelton on *Clontarf* and joined a relative on a farm now known as Patoka Station, about thirty miles from Napier. Two years later Mr Sealy entered the survey department in Hawke's Bay, and after four years came to Canterbury, as district surveyor. He bought the Rockwood estate in the Tengawai district, and farmed it for about five years, and also acquired the Ellerslie estate, near Geraldine. He was married in 1873 to a daughter of Mr T. Sanderson, a well known North Canterbury runholder, and had five daughters and one son.

Triggs, James. Born in Suffolk 1859, he arrived on the *Clontarf* with his wife Sarah Ann and their two year old son Robert. James bought a farm just west of the railway crossing at Papanui next door to Henry Matson's estate "Delce." He worked as a dairy farmer and later grew fruit trees. He supplemented his income by working for St. Paul's church and in the 1870s was the 'beloved verger.'

Turner, Charles and Mary Ann. Married in 1845 in West Yorkshire, Charles and Mary-Ann came to New Zealand on the *Clontarf* with their four children in hopes of Charles working as a gardener or brick maker. Mary's child, a girl, was stillborn on the voyage. They remained in the Canterbury area and lived very long lives. Charles dying on the 18th of July 1917 aged 95yrs and Mary Ann 3rd of May 1908 aged 83yrs. Both are buried at the Harewood St James Anglican Church, in Christchurch.

George Woodhead jnr

Woodhead, *George Junior*. Mr G. Woodhead was born in Nottingshire, England in 1844 and accompanied his parents in *Clontarf*. With his father he established Manor Farm, which was near Temuka. He was a member of the St George's Lodge of Freemasons, Temuka. In 1892 he married Miss Longson of Glossop, Derbyshire, England but they had no children.

George Woodhead Snr

Woodhead, *George Senior*, was born in Nottinghamshire, England in 1811 and brought out his wife and family to New Zealand in *Clontarf*. For about four years he was employed at the Rakaia Gorge and Selwyn. Then he went to Cashmere, near Christchurch, and took up a farm which he kept for three years. In 1866 he leased a farm near Temuka from the late Mr Hayhurst, and worked it with his son for 21 years. On the expiration of the lease they bought a place at Milford, near Temuka, and named it Manor Farm.

Passengers 1858-59

Voyage Two

Nov 30th 1859 – March 16th 1860

ARTHUR WILLIS, GANN, AND CO.'S
LINE OF PACKETS
BETWEEN
LONDON AND NEW ZEALAND.

THE following fine first-class Ships are intended to be continued as Regular Traders.

Ships.	Commanders.	Tons.
Zealandia	J. Foster	1800
Caduceus	J. Cass	1600
Clontarf	A. W. Barclay	1600
Egmont	S. C. Gibson	1200
Maori	C. G. Petherbridge	1200
Joseph Fletcher	J. Pook	1000
Cushmere	J. Byron	1000
Cresswell	W. C. Barrett	1000
Hastings	C. Cowie	1000
Strathallan	W. Williamson	1000
Harwood	W. Forsayth	800

The Undersigned Agents for the above splendid Line of Vessels, are authorised to arrange with Settlers here, who may be desirous of bringing their Friends in Great Britain out to this Colony, and are prepared either to pay the Passage Money at once, or give satisfactory security for payment on arrival of the Vessel.

Further particulars may be known by applying to
BETHUNE & HUNTER.
January 6, 1860.

Wellington Independent Newspaper Jan 1860

Gravesend in the nineteenth century, published in William Gaspey, "Tallis's Illustrated London"

𝓡ight from the outset *Clontarf* and her passengers on the 1859-60 voyage seemed to have stepped under a gloomy cloud of misfortune. Heavy weather hit as they boarded at Gravesend and prevailed while they were piloted down the Thames and into the channel. It was four days before the weather broke and they got the chance to meet each other on deck. The calm was short lived though and the seas began to batter them once more as they entered the Bay of Biscay.

On Tuesday Dec 6th the storm winds damaged the mizen top sail and marooned the ship and passengers in the Bay of Biscay. Sea-sickness was rampant, and hopes for a speedy exit from the Bay were fleeting. Capt. Barclay declared to his crew if the weather did not relent they would turn back for England. But it was too late. On Dec 8th the heavens opened up and the eye of the storm hit them violently. Breakfast was just being consumed when surging seas smashed the bulwarks (an extension of a ship's sides above the level of the deck) and broke into the decking house, filling all the cabins with water. Everything was saturated; bedding, clothing, and everyone's belongings. The passengers, regardless of class, were set to "bucket and pails" and it was well into the night before the water was removed. Then the poor weary passengers, who were unable to retire to their soaking beds, had to find comfort sleeping where they could. Due to conditions only a single meal was provided for them that whole day.

Finally the storm seemed to be over. The next day was calm and the sail was quickly fixed. The winds picked up to get them out of the cursed Bay of Biscay. It was then that the Captain made the ill fated decision to continue; the break in the weather invigorated everyone's hopes and the ship made good speed.

Riding the Trade Winds

Once *Clontarf* caught the trade winds she was whisked along at 8 to 12 knots. She was now no longer isolated as other ships fell in alongside her and rode the winds with her. Records indicate these ships would often communicate and swap supplies with each other en-route. The warm wind from the tropics saw the crew and passengers basking in the sun and, for a time, everyone seemed happy.

Dec 9th was when the first signs of illness appeared on *Clontarf*. Two children were sent to the ship's hospital, which was under the care of the ships medical officer, Doctor Stone. He diagnosed the sickly children with measles. This seemed fairly normal and routine; and although Stone knew there would likely be more cases, he put it down to what one might expect on such a voyage.

Shortly afterwards, a brawl erupted below decks in the Single-men's quarters between an Irish family called the Smarts, Dr Stone himself, a "large Scottish man" and a handful of other passengers. It started with one of the Smart family being accused of having lice. Dr Stone ordered the Scotsman, who was a barber by trade, to shave the young man's head. While this was under-way some of the other members of the Smart family took offence to being perceived as 'lousey' and jumped the Scotsman. Two Englishmen tried to intervene in the skirmish and before long an all out war erupted with combatants using broomsticks and crowbars. Many men were badly wounded. The captain arrived with his officers and the constable in tow and threatened to put them all in irons, to which the antagonist Mr Smart, father of the young men, promptly threatened to kill everyone on board the ship. To this the Scotsman, who was described as

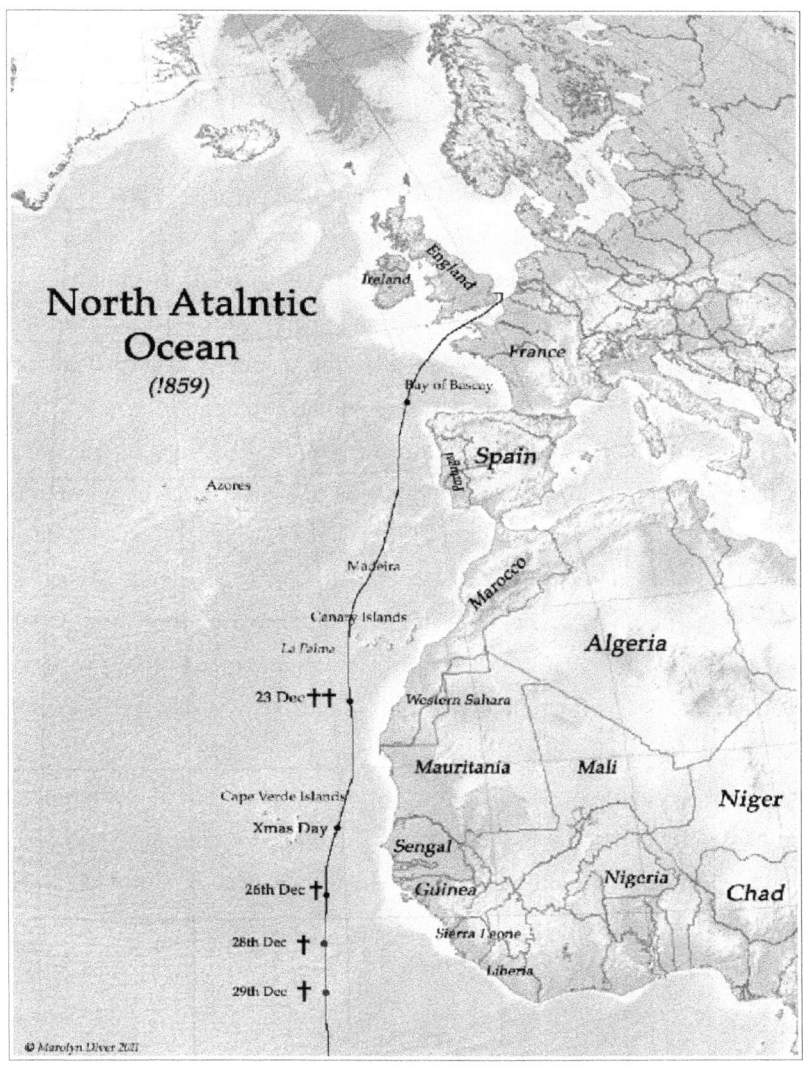

"a brawny man", punched Smart so hard it knocked him unconscious. The captain conveniently ignored the Scotsman's retaliation and threatened the remaining Smarts that they will be brought up on charges once on land if they didn't behave. It seemed to do the trick as all went back to normal shortly afterwards.

On the week of the 18th of December the ship passed by Madeira with the vessel *Frenchman* settling in as a sailing companion as she travelled from Liverpool to Adelaide. By this time the hospital was full of children – one record estimated 32. Nevertheless Dr Stone took it in his stride and tended to them all. At the same time he dealt with the passenger's normal aliments; tropical heat stroke, tooth ache, and even Moon-Stroke "from too much time spend under the full moon!" The full moon must have bought out unusual behaviours in more than a few as Chief Cabin passenger Mr Plunket went on a drinking binge and caused a tremendous ruckus. The skipper ordered him off the deck and had him confined to his room. A pig lightened the mood somewhat by strangely committing suicide by running through a porthole and plunging into the sea. But this would be the last of the merriment. For on the night of Thursday Dec 23nd two children passed away in the ship's hospital. Elizabeth Parker aged six months and Benjamin Waller 12 months. The captain read a service at dusk and committed the bodies to the deep while the ship gathered solemnly with lanterns and sung hymns. It was a fitting send off for the children, all grieved the tragic loss of these young lives then wandered off to their quarters to reflect on the cruelty of nature. Soon things returned to normal.

Christmas

As Christmas Day approached the hot weather became almost unbearable for the passengers. They slept in near nakedness and sheltered below to escape the midday sun. While at first the passengers had loved the change from the English winter they had just left, the temperatures soared and the humidity very soon turned their pleasure into misery.

Christmas dinner was served between the Cape De Verde Islands and the coast of Africa. A canvas was strung over the poop deck to shadow the passengers and crew, who basked in the warm tropical breeze under the blissful shade. They celebrated the day with great joy. But the next day, like a ominous sign from above, the trade winds abruptly stopped.

The three ships that had travelled beside *Clontarf* also became dead in the water in the unbearable heat. To top it off a child died during the night, Samuel Allen, aged three years. He died from what was to become a regular diagnosis; convulsions bought on by whooping cough or measles. With the wind gone, the seas deadly still, illness began to intensify, not only in children but adults too. The ships doctor and captain also began to show signs of sickness with a large part of the crew already down. On the 28th Dec, Charles Jones died aged 2½, followed the next day by William Mitton also 2 ½ and an unnamed daughter of crew member Mrs Sinclair.

With New Years Eve came the death of Lucy Faries, who was 18 months old. By now the three ships that sailed close to *Clontarf* had learned from regular signalling of the ships unfolding tragedy. They lowered their flags in respect and some, like the Swedish ship *Sophia,* manoeuvred along side *Clontarf* during the funerals to be a part of the services. A touching gesture from strangers in the middle of the ocean.

The Swedish ship Sophia *in dock. While traveling next to* Clontarf *she came abreast and lowered her main sails during the children's funerals*

By all accounts Dr Stone was beginning to understand the underlining cause of the illness, which in most cases were looking less and less like measles or whooping cough and more like malaria and typhoid; especially in the adults. He ordered all the passengers to bring their belongings on deck, still heavily waterlogged from the storm in the Bay of Biscay. The heat, damp and close quarters of so many people was a breeding ground for all kinds of rampant illness. Dr Stone became, quite rightly, tyrannical about drying everything. As one passenger argued with him about the regimental ordering of the passengers to dry their possessions on the deck for the second time, stress got the better of him. He replied angrily to the accusation of treating them like animals with *"Yes, you are considered as such, and I did not know you had the right to think!"* which did not sit well with those who heard it. *"Fine words for a gentleman,"* one passenger wrote in disgust. But poor Dr Stone was carrying the fate of the ship on his shoulders. Children in the hospital were fading quickly, adults were dropping like flies, and he himself was getting sicker by the hour. The passengers may not have known what was about to hit them, but records suggest that Dr Stone was aware of the tragedy that was about to befall the ship.

Shortly after New Year the trade winds returned. A small blessing, for at least now the stagnation was over. She shifted with the other ships into the S.E winds. However now moving again the deaths did not abate. Two more children passed away on 3rd of January. Three days later was the first adult death. An Irish midshipman named Stokes aged 18 died of "brain fever" from excessive drinking.

He had drunk himself into unconsciousness on Christmas Day and never recovered. A tragic and unnecessary waste of life. In the few days that followed a child died almost every day, some days marked the passing of two children.

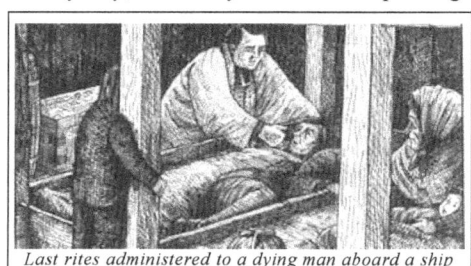
Last rites administered to a dying man aboard a ship

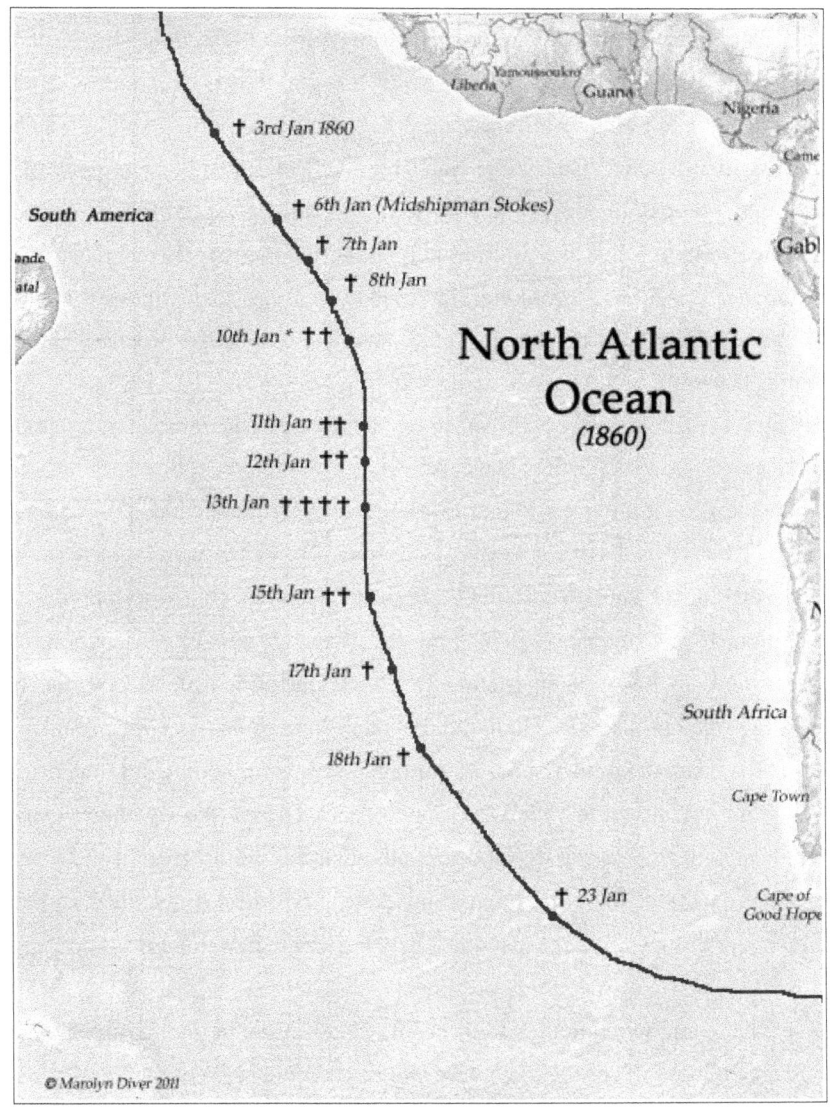

The Darkest Of Days

The worst day was to fall on Friday the 13th of January. Four children died and the ship fell into a great dark period of hopelessness.

In a diary entry on this day William Perkins wrote "*The people seem to think the ship is doomed and have all lost heart.*" It was poignant that on this day Dr Stone succumbed to his own illness, thought to be consumption, and he was not expected to last long. Their final hope for medical salvation was gone. The ships that companioned *Clontarf* looked on with great empathy, offering assistance from afar but they were as helpless as the passengers and the crew in the doomed ship itself. More children died on the days that followed. On the 16th a small glimmer of hope arrived with the birth of a baby boy called George Clontarf Burrows. Sadly he was to die just 16 days later.

By now the Captain was confined to his quarters, as too were a large number of the crew. The First Officer took control, but confusion and instability hung over the ship. Children continued to die; George Walters aged 12 months on the 17th, Mary Ann Berry, 4 years old on the 23rd. Then came another adult death; Mr Plunket the half-fare navy officer in Second Cabin who had taken it upon himself to remain as drunk and as rowdy as possible throughout the voyage died. In his weakened state Dr Stone performed an autopsy on Mr Plunket to rule out diseases. He found the man's liver to be twice its normal size and put his death down to alcohol poisoning. Yet another adult lost to the drink.

As *Clontarf* moved to round the Cape of Good Hope the weather changed dramatically. It cooled rapidly and the sub-antarctic winds greeted them with fury. The deaths of the children continued steadily, but did not intensify, and the numbers dropped back to just one a day. On some days there were no deaths at all.

A setback came with another adult death, Eliza Barton, a young woman aged 19. She had fallen ill some time before and died on the night of the 7th. By now Dr Stone was far too sick to perform an autopsy; but since Miss Barton was a gentle lady without a passion for the drink, it was thought that she had died from one of the many illness that took the children and laid up so many adults on board.

The Captain was too sick to hold the funeral for Miss Burton, so the First Officer had to reassure the passengers that the worst was over and Miss Burton's death was due to her slight build and pre-disposition to illness. Few believed him as she was seen fit and healthy only weeks ago. To add to the worry, on the very same day the Constable fell down an open hatch and fractured his skull. Dr Stone tended to him in such a weak state that he was unable to dress himself.

Onwards into the Indian Ocean

10th February. With the heat of the topics behind them and the Cape of Good Hope rounding surprisingly calm and clear, *Clontarf* was finally making good time. The passengers were now forced to contend with the cold. Icy winds and snow besieged them; mists were so thick the other ships were impossible to see; squalls battered her from every angle. Icebergs, a rarity for the passengers, had everyone clambering onto the deck in bitterly cold conditions to view them. The First Officer took bearings of one and noted it was three miles long! Large chunks of ice surrounded the ship at times, slowing their speed somewhat as the crew spent time navigating them carefully. Captain Barclay's health slowly began to improve and he made painful efforts to appear on deck to reassure the passengers. This seemed to work well; most diaries record the days he made an appearance and how a calm would descend over the ship during those times. Meanwhile as the ship passed Prince Edward Islands and moved upward to Kerguelen Island, the trip was almost three-quarters done. Dr Stone was not expected to live to reach New Zealand.

Artic Ship Valorous Albert From The Illustrated London News 1850

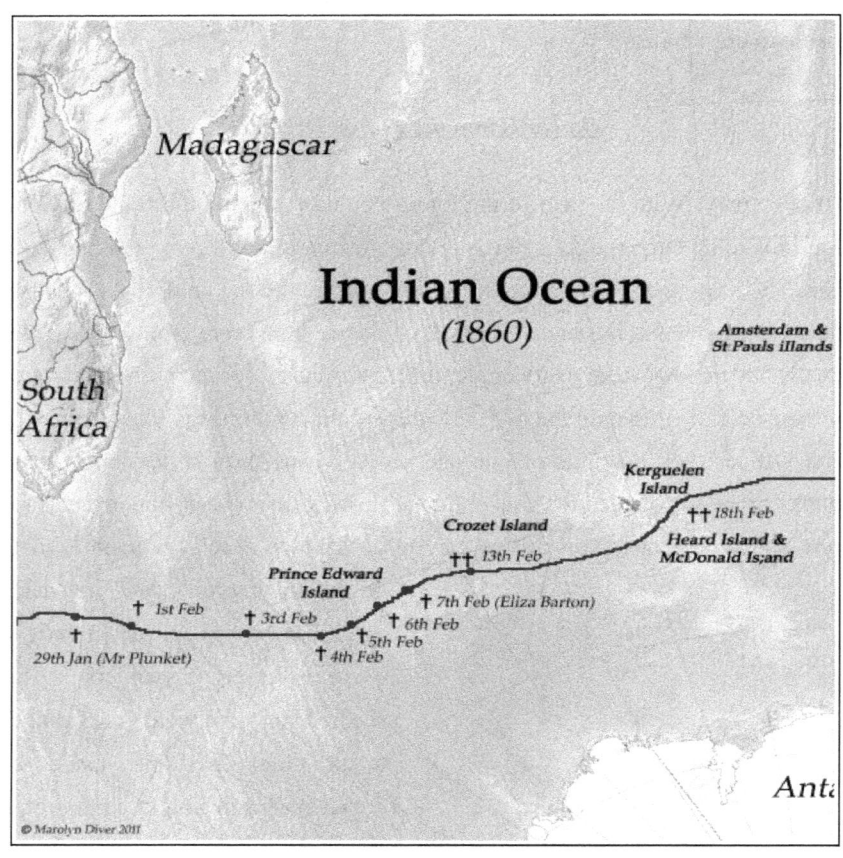

Voyage Two

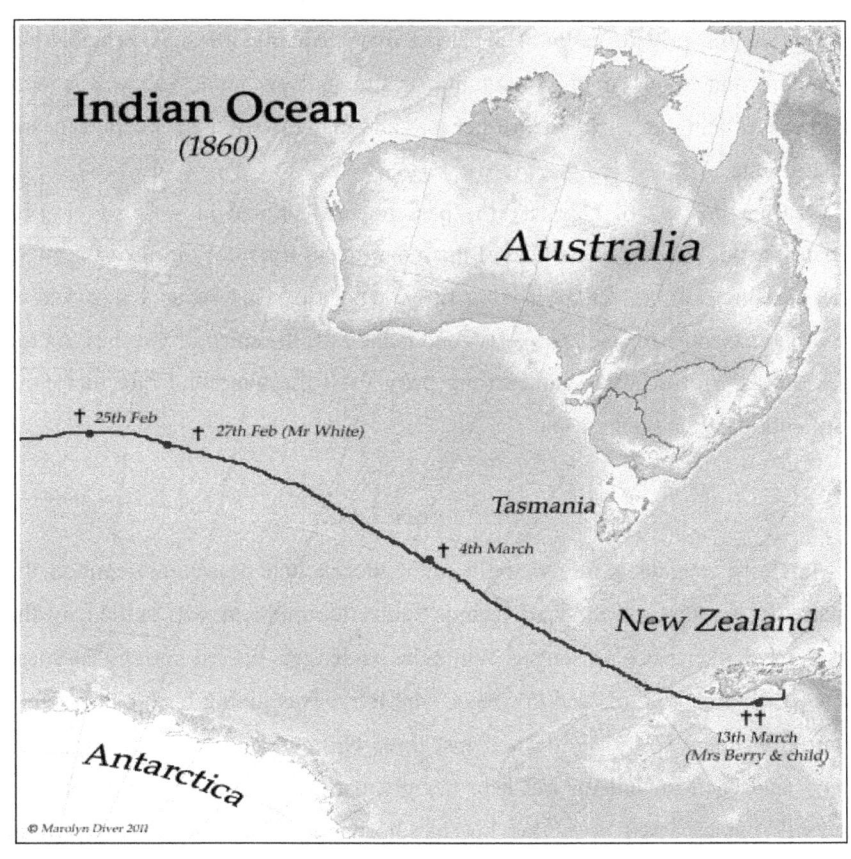

On the 27th of February, and so close to the end of the voyage, Chief Passenger Mr White died. He had married his bride just one week before boarding the *Clontarf* in England and was moving to New Zealand for his health. He suffered from "Putrid Throat" which at the time could have been one of a wide range of illness - possibly even diphtheria which was highly contagious. Unfortunately he became bedridden soon after boarding and spent most of the voyage in his private cabin. He passed away leaving his new bride alone, pregnant, and about to disembark into a strange new land. She was widely reported as being inconsolable for her loss and many passengers worried for her mental state.

Nearing the end of February the passengers delighted in seeing their first albatross south of Australia. One of the magnificent migratory birds was caught and measured at 11 feet from wing tip to wing tip. This became a source of great wonderment for the passengers and helped lift the spirit of the ship. As too was the birth of a healthy and strong baby. All the wind and rain to follow could not dampen their spirits.

The Promised Land

March 13th, under a fine moonlit night the excited passengers spotted the Snares Rocks just off Steward Island. Sadly this moment was sullied by the death of another adult passenger. While the passengers peered into the darkness to see their first sign of land in weeks, Mrs Berry was giving birth below deck. The unfortunate Berry family had lost three children on the voyage and Mrs Berry had been unwell for much of her pregnancy. During the night both her and her baby passed away leaving her husband and remaining children in mourning as they entered New Zealand waters.

The next day the passengers got their first view of the mainland from the deck. They would have marvelled at the rough coastline and vast expanses of forests as they sailed by. The sparsely populated coastal settlements were in sharp contrast to the sprawling smoggy cities and towns of industrial England.

As the day wore on they would have watched the rolling hills smooth into the expansive Canterbury Plains with Banks Peninsula rising in the distance to greet them.

They arrived in Lyttelton Harbour on the 16th of March, and there was a long collective sigh of relief.

"Scarcely a ripple stirred the waters of the Harbour of Port Lyttelton as, on the 16th of March 1860, the good ship Clontarf, lay off the heads waiting for the pilot to come on board.

Leaning over the stern of the vessel, I gazed upon the features of the new land which I had adopted, and, after 107 days of ocean surroundings, I was fain to regard the strange country with feelings of pleasure, indeed I can still recall the desire which stirred with in me to get ashore and to roll on the verdant turf, which looked so fresh and lovely after the long voyage - a feeling which I have heard expressed by others who have been for months at sea, deprived of the sight of trees, grass, and flowers.

A boat put off from the pilot station at last, and, manned by a Maori crew, it seemed to skim over the smooth surface as easily as did the many gulls and sea-fowl which were flying around shrieking their plaintive cries, and quarrelling over any stray morsel that dropped over board.

On the quarter-deck and on the forecastle groups of steerage were standing by the bulwarks and hanging on the rattlings, expressing their opinions on the appearance of the land: and I saw a good many tears shed, as some of the doubtless remembered that they would soon have to part from the good ship that had been their home for so long. Not that the voyage had been one of unalloyed bliss, unmarred by any melancholy event-death had thinned our ranks considerably, thirty-six* of our numbers having been taken away, a circumstance which gained for the Clontarf the questionable honour of being mentioned in the future New Zealand almanacs, the death rate during the voyage having beaten all previous records."

Chief Passenger Alfred H. Duncan

"Early Days in New Zealand 1888"

*The final death toll was in-fact 41, including newborn babies.

A Troubled End

Once piloted into Lyttelton the passengers and crew were cleared by the harbour doctor, but it was to be a few days before they left the ship completely. Often passengers spent a night or two back on the ship while they packed up and found alternative accommodation on shore. 20 passengers were set to remain with *Clontarf* and travel down to Timaru and Otago, then back up to Wellington. But this was not to be the case.

On returning to the ship the passengers found several crew clamped in irons, waiting to be escorted to shore. These crew members were refusing to continue with *Clontarf*. They had actively voiced their unhappiness to the Captain about being refused time to recover from the disastrous voyage before setting sail again. Others had simply announced they were leaving and wanted nothing more to do with the "doomed" ship.

In the end they all got their wish, one way or another. The Lyttelton police were called for and the mutineers were arrested and put in jail for "Refusing to carry out their Duties." Six other crew members were to follow them in the following days. This left only a handful of loyal men and the Captain was forced to make plans to sail off without them. Due to the frustrating delays the remaining passengers decided to leave *Clontarf* as well, opting to take mail steamships or coaches to their final destinations. Short-handed it took a painfully long time to unload her cargo and, as a result, *Clontarf* was forced to abandon sailing to the other New Zealand ports altogether. Instead they employed the ship *Fanny A. Garrigues* to take over her cargo delivery.

On a skeleton crew she readied for the return home and on the 11th of May, with full ballast and only two passengers on board she left Lyttelton harbour, never to return to New Zealand again.

Dr Stones' condition, or if he survived his illness, seems not to have been recorded once the *Clontarf* arrived in New Zealand. One might speculate that he was possibly taken to Lyttelton hospital where he may have finally succumbed to his illness and died. If so, it would make the unwavering, heroic and tragic Dr Stone one of the final unrecorded victims of the *Clontarf* and her horrific voyage of 1859-60.

Deaths and Births

Deaths
1859

23th December:	Elizabeth Parker, 6 months.
	Benjamin Waller, 12 months.
26th December:	Samuel Allen, 2 years old.
28th December:	Charles Jones, 3 years old.
29th December:	James Richie, 2 years old.
30th December:	William Mitton, 2 years old.
31th December:	Lucy Emma Faires, 18 months.

1860

3rd January:	Robert Hargood, 6 years old.
6th January:	Mr Stokes, Midshipman. 18 years.
7th January:	Amelia Wright, 11 months.
8th January:	Elizabeth Wilkinson. 7 years old.
10th January:	Son of Passengers Cook. Crew member.*
	Son of Mr Steward, Crew member.*
11th January:	Robert J. Cargill Waller, 5 years old.
	Thomas Sadler. 3 years old.
12th January:	Son of Mr McDonald, Crew member.*
	Daughter of Mr Aldroft.*
13th January:	Martha Judson, 7 months old.
	Besty Sadler. 11 months old
	Thomas Burrows, 2 years old.
	Ellen Berry, 1year old.
15th January:	Maria Hawthron, 1 year old.
	Emily Mitton, 11 months old.
17th January:	George John Walters, 12 months.
18th January:	Unnamed Child.*
23rd January:	Mary Ann Berry, 4 years old.
29th January:	Mr W. Plunket, aged 23 years old.
1st February:	Ellen Bloomfield, 10 months old.
3rd February:	Amy Eliza Seager, 2 years old.
4th February:	George Clontarf Burrows, 16 days old.
6th February:	Ellen Ashman, 8 years old.
7th February:	Miss Eliza Barton, 19 years old.
13th February:	Son of Steerage passenger Mrs Cook died.*
	Margaret Begg, 12 months old.
18th February:	Henry Rouse, 7 years old.
	George Henry Carr, 2 years old.
25th February:	Charlotte Hargood. 4 years old.
27th February:	Mr White, aged 26 years old.
4th March:	Baby of Mrs Wright, born 5th of Feb died.
13th March:	Mrs Berry, aged 31 years old.
	Baby of Mrs Berry, died 3 hours old.

41 deaths in total.

*Deaths/ Births mentioned in more than one personal account, though not in official news papers death list.

Births

16th January:	Birth. George Clontarf Burrows.
25th February:	Baby born. Unnamed*
5th February:	Baby Born to Mrs Wright
11th March:	Baby Born to Mrs Hawthorn,
13th March:	Baby of Mrs Berry

Clontarf Cargo

TO ARRIVE IN THE CLONTARF:

120 kegs Ewbank's and French wire nails
9 bundles Lyndon's spades and shovels
60 boxes crown glass
23 boxes plate glass
12 iron pillar pumps
5 casks cable and coil chain
12 reams brown paper
1 10-ton weighing machine
1 case electro-plate cruet frames
3 casks tinware
28 barrels gunpowder
8 cases fenders
1 case fire irons
7 cases Kent and Wood grates
18 Register stoves
12 kitchen ranges
3 patent anvils
3 P. Smith's bellows, with backs and tue irons
9½ tons bar iron and 6 bundles hoops
1 bundle (L) blister steel
9 casks bolts and nuts, and 1 cask washers
10 bundles sheet iron
1 cask files
1 cask shot and 1 cask zinc
100 gallons colza oil
1 cask coffin furniture
6 bundles pig lattice wire work
3 cases looking glasses.
           E. REECE & CO.,
             Oxford Street, Lyttelton.

Clontarf Cargo 1859-60

SAILED.

May 24, ship Clontarf, 1100 tons, Barclay, for Callao, in ballast. Passengers — Messrs. Mallock and Walker.

Lyttelton Times 26 May 1860.

Passengers Testimonials

(Lyttelton Times March 23rd 1860)

"Ship Clontarf, March 14, 1860.
"To A. W. BARCLAY, Esq., Commander.
"DEAR SIR,—We the undersigned saloon passengers of the ship Clontarf, bound from the port of London to that of Lyttelton, N.Z., cannot take leave of you without expressing the great regard we entertain for and the sympathy we feel toward you.

"Though adverse to a general system of testimonial letters on the conclusion of voyages, and judging you a man of too high a character to be anxious to receive any such from us, yet on this occasion we hope to be allowed to express the very great admiration your conduct during this trying voyage has raised in us.

"Throughout this voyage, in misfortunes so unprecedented, your powers, both mental and physical, have been severely tested; yet harrassed with severe weather, worn out with anxiety for and attention to your emigrants, we have ever received at your hands the greatest kindness and consideration.

"We wish you a safe return home, and with every prayer for your future happiness, we subscribe ourselves

"Yours very sincerely."
(Signed by C. PERCY SOULSBY, and 10 others.)

Chief and Second Cabin Passengers Patronage

[From the Single Women.]
"Ship Clontarf, March 15th, 1860.
"To CAPTAIN BARCLAY.
"SIR,—We, the undersigned, steerage passengers by the ship Clontarf, from London to New Zealand, feel now that our journey is accomplished that we cannot leave without taking this our only means of thanking you for the great kindness and attention we have received from you and your officers during our long and trying passage.

"During the time we have been under your charge, you have always shown yourself ready to attend to the wants and comforts of all classes of passengers, and those who have been ill amongst us will always remember with gratitude the valuable services rendered by the doctor and yourself. Trusting you will have a prosperous voyage home,

"We remain your obedient servants."
(Signed by MRS. CURD, Matron, and 25 single women)

Single Woman's patronage.

Passengers 1859-60

Passengers 1859-60

Passengers 1859-60

(In Alphbetical Order)

Butterfield, John and Sarah

John Butterfield and his four daughters & eight sons Circa.1900 Courtesy of Lindsay Butterfield.

John Butterfield was born in Ilkley, Yorkshire on the 15th February 1829. In 1859 he married Sarah (Thompson) and in the same year they emigrated to N.Z. After leaving *Clontarf* they moved to Burwood, Christchurch and John took up the occupation as milkman. It was here that their first three children were born. After this they shifted to Russells Flat just out of Springfield where John worked as a farm labourer and 10 more children were to follow. Sarah died of cancer in 1887 while John died of a heart attack in 1915. They are both buried in the Springfield Cemetery.

Coatman, Joseph and Mary of Ely, Cambridgeshire. Their three children accompanied them on the voyage to New Zealand along with children from Mary's first marriage. They were lucky to not suffer any fatalities. However another daughter only shown on the registry as Charlotte Coatman was later left out of the final shipping list, leading to speculation that she died just before they boarded and the death was not registered at that time. After emigrating they settled at Woodend, Joseph working on roads which entitled him to a small land grant, which they farmed until their deaths.

Dearnaley, Edwin and Sarah. Edwin was born in 1828 at Tintwistle, Cheshire, England and married Sarah (*nee* Moore) born in 1856 at Ecclesall Bierlow, Yorkshire, England. A carpenter by trade they emigrated to New Zealand and moved to Selwyn, Canterbury where they had one son. Edwin died aged 62 on the 22nd of December 1892 while Sarah died 5 years later aged 70. They are both buried at Springton Cemetery.

Double, Robert and Harriet. Robert and Harriet took passage on the *Clontarf* with their baby daughter Ann and travelled afterwards to Timaru. There they opened a boarding house and had nine more children. Harriet died 29 Apr 1915 while Robert died on 17 Dec 1919 both residing in Invercargill.

Early, Stephen was born in 1840, at Ringwood, Hampshire, England, and educated and brought up as a builder by his father. He arrived in Lyttelton on *Clontarf* having written a diary of his voyage on the ship. He was married in 1862 and had four sons and five daughters. He was for a short time in business with his father in Christchurch, and then he the held the position of Postmaster at Cust, Canterbury for two years. In 1864 he began a business as a general storekeeper, a baker and undertaker. He carried on the store for eighteen years.

Frame, James. James was a native of Lanark, Scotland, where he was born in 1844. After his voyage on the *Clontarf* at the age of 16 with his family, he spent a short time in Otago during the Gabriel's Gully "gold rush." He then joined the railway under the Provincial Government in 1872 as a shunter at Christchurch and worked his way through the various grades of the service to become stationmaster at Addington Junction Railway Station Lincoln in 1874. Mr Frame was married in 1863 to another Scotland native, and had two sons and three daughters.

Mr & Mrs Galletly

Galletly, John. Mr Galletly was born in Perthshire, Scotland in 1840, and was brought up with outdoor pursuits. In 1860 he landed in Lyttelton. After working for a year at Kaiapoi Island, and three years on the Riccarton estate, he bought fifty acres of land in the Cust district on which his homestead stood. He married a Miss Shea, of County Tipperary, Ireland, and had two sons and two daughters

Judson, James. Mr Judson was born in 1847, in Leicestershire, England. After departing *Clontarf* he gained experience in farming and began his own farm at Woodend in 1870. For 15 years he also acted as librarian and treasurer of the local library. Mr Judson was married in 1869 and had three sons and five daughters.

Jabez Lord

Lord, Jabez was born in Sowerby near Halifax, Yorkshire, England. He married Mary Ann Spencer. They left England the same month as their wedding and sailed to New Zealand on the *Clontarf*. He bought a small farm in the Courtenay district near Racecourse Hill where he went in for wool carting and had eight sons and two daughters. He died on the 10th of May 1924 at the age of 87 and was buried in Linwood Cemetery with his wife, Mary.

Rouse, James and Maria sailed along with their eight children on the *Clontarf* from Blythburgh, Suffolk, England. Maria was pregnant throughout the voyage and they suffered the loss of their youngest boy Henry, age seven, wrongly recorded as 'Mary' on the death list. They managed to arrive in New Zealand relatively unscathed from the voyage. On the 1st of April 1860 Maria gave birth to a son in Lyttelton and called him Henry after his older brother who died at sea. Baby Henry died at only 14 hours old. Six days later Maria died of dysentery at Lyttelton Hospital on 7 April 1860 aged 37 years old and was buried in the Lyttelton Cemetery with her son.

> THE Father and Mother of a Family named ROUSE, who arrived in the Clontarf, have lately died, leaving seven children. Persons desirous of assisting these orphans are invited to transmit the sums they may collect to the care of the Rev. B. W. DUDLEY, at Rangiora, April 16, 1860.

A charitable advert placed in the Lyttelton Times. May 16th 1860

James took the surviving seven children to Rangiora, Canterbury. But only one month after arriving in New Zealand and nine days after their mother died, the children's father also passed away on the 16th April 1860 aged 39 years old in Rangiora, leaving the seven children orphans.

Sadler, Thomas and Sarah. On the *Clontarf* two of Thomas and Sarah's three children died on the voyage along with Sarah's sister Eliza Barton who was 19 years old. The Sadler family settled in Templeton not far from Christchurch. There they purchased a farm and had several more children. Both Thomas and Sarah Sadler were buried at Templeton in the Church Cemetery.

John Sheehan

Sheehan, John was born at Nenagh, Tipperary, Ireland in 1850. In 1860 aged 10 years he accompanied his parents to New Zealand in *Clontarf*. After attending school in Christchurch, he was first employed to drive a team of horses and afterwards worked at a threshing machine for seven years. Mr Sheehan then began farming and for 27 years carried on successfully at Tai Tapu. He was married twice; firstly, to Miss Doyle, by whom there was a family of five children, and secondly, to Miss Flynn, who gave him two sons and five daughters.

Waller, William & Jane of Edinburgh. Shipping information would claim that William and Jane were husband and wife, though descendants have found that Jane's husband had in fact jumped ship from his duties in New Zealand a year beforehand and William was perhaps his brother escorting his sister-in-law and young family. William was employed on the ship as a crew member and would have received a greatly reduced fare for his "family" to accompany him. Unfortunately only one of Jane's three children survived the journey.

White, Mr & Mrs (Mistakenly written as Wright on passenger list). Married just four days before boarding *Clontarf* as Chief Cabin Passengers. They were moving to a better climate for Mr White's failing health which was diagnosed as *putrid throat* (possibly diphtheria which is highly contagious). Sadly his health deteriorated immediately and on the 27th of February he passed away, leaving his pregnant wife a widow coming to a new land. In shipboard diaries she was described as understandably distraught and inconsolable. The fate of both her and her unborn child in New Zealand is unknown.

Passengers 1859-60

Passenger List 1858-59

Passenger List 1858-59

Passenger List 1858-59

Chief Cabin Passengers	Name	Age	Location	Occupation/Notes
Acland	John Barton	23		
Bennett	Joseph Henry			
Blakely	Jane and George			
Burnell	Edward			
Cooper	Georgina			
	Charlotte			
	Sarah			
	Arthur Robert			
Jollie	Francis			
Lock	James Carnegy			
Riddell	Walter			
Sealy	Edward Percy	26		
Second Cabin	Name	Age	Location	Occupation/Notes
Badely	Edward			
Brake	John			
	Wife, 4 children			
Kinnibrook	David			
Raddon	Lewis		Somerset	
	Wife, 2 children			
Paying Steerage Passengers				
Murray	Sarah		Somerset	Daughters of Mrs Raddon
	Mary Ann			

		Elizabeth			
	Batt	Wm			
	Granger	Thomas B.			
		George W.			
	Grigg	Edward F			
	Hartnell	George W			
	Phillips	William Henry			
	Voisin	John Phillip			
Assisted Passengers		*Families & Children*	*Age*	*Location*	*Occupation/Notes*
	Ashton	Sampson	22		Labourer
		Rachel	21		Boot-maker
	Atkinson	John	46		
		Margaret	43		
		John	20	Trans to Single Men	
		Margaret	18	Trans to Single Women	
		Henry	16	Trans to Single Men	
		Richard	13	Trans to Single Men	
		Francis	9		
		Eliza	7		
		Kendal	4		
		Twins (Kate & Unnamed)	8m		***Kate-Died at sea 22/11/1858***
	Brake	John	43		Cooper
		Lucy	41		
		Henry Peach	12		

		Harriet Georgina	9		
		Robert	7		
		Mary Charlotte	3		*(Died in NZ harbour 05/01/1859)*
	Beal	Henry	27		Gardener
		Mary	30		
		William	5		
		Mark	2		
	Billens	Robert	39		Tinsmith
		Caroline	38		
		Frederick	14		
		Henry	12		
		Louisa	10		
		Lucy	6		
		Emma	4		
		Robert	2		
	Blythe	William	29		
		Jane	25		Farm Servant
	Broome	Thomas	28		Labourer
		Hannah	24		
		David	8m		
	Brown	John Ellson	33		Printer & Bookbinder
		Mary E	22		
		Jane E	2		
	Brown	Frederick	28		Farm labourer
		Mary Ann	25		
		Clara	5		

		William Henry	1		
Bryan		Isaac	25		Labourer
		Ann	26		
Buckley		Henry	34		Gardener
		Eliza	35		
		Mary E	11		
		Eliza Ann	9		
		James	7		
		John	4		
		Baby	1		
Cain		John	46		Farm Labourer
		Sarah	43		
		Hanse	16	Trans to Single Men	Agriculturalist
		David	14	Trans to Single Men	
		Mary	12	Trans to Singe Woman	
		Samuel	10		
		James	8		
		Agnes	4		
Chapman		William	37		Agricultural Labourer
		Wife	35		
		James	16	Trans to Single Men	Agricultural Labourer
		William	13	Trans to Single Men	Agricultural Labourer
		Betsey	10		

		Ann	6		
		Thomas	4		
		Mary	1		
	Clark	Christopher	41		Wheelwright
		Hannah	39		
	Clark	Richard	39		Labourer
		Ellen	32		
		William	12		
		Hannah	10		
		Elisha	1		*Died at sea (28/10/58)*
	Cole	John	60		Miller
		Elizabeth	61		
	Dudson	William	33		Labourer
		Margaret	30		
		Thomas	6		
		Mary	4		
		Francis	3		
		Walter	1 m		
	Duff	John	32		Ploughman
		Letitia	34		
		Robert	8		
		Margaret	2		
		Mary	Infant		
	Dulien	Richard	37		Labourer
		Elizabeth	33		
		Richard	10		
	Elliott	Henry	40		Labourer

	Amelia	44		
	Henrietta	7		
Ellis	Joseph	28		Bricklayer
	Martha	26		
	Godfrey	5		
	Elizabeth	1		
	Susannah	Inf		*Born and died at sea. 28/10/58 (18 days old.)*
Elms	William	19		Gardener
Evans	Edward	29		Agricultural Labourer
	Ann	23		***Died at sea 24/11/1858***
Fabian	William James	29		Carpenter
	Elizabeth Jane	25		
Gapes	William	34		Carman/Labourer
	Esther	32		
	Esther	14	Trans to Single Woman	
	Maria	10		
	EMMA	2		
Gibson	Benjamin	21		Labourer
	Elizabeth	25		
Glendenning	Elizabeth	18		
Gordon	Henry	32		Farm Servant
	Jessie	27		
	William	5		
Gracey	William	34		Labourer
	Margaret	27		

		Alexander	infant		
Greig		Alexander	25		Millwright & Carpenter
		Isabella	22		
Hampton		James	25		Ploughman
		Margaret	12		
		Ann1	1		
Harkess		Thomas	36		Carpenter
		Elizabeth	31		
		Thomas	3		
		Elizabeth Ann	7m		
Healy		John	33		Farm Labourer
		Leah	23		
		Mary	3		
		George	6m		
Hibbett		William			
		And Family			
Horner		William	24		Blacksmith
		Mary	22		
		James William	2		
Howard		George	35		
		Harriett	38		
		Margaret			
Jennings		Charles	32		Schoolmaster
		Jane	29		
		Jane M	4		
		Mary	2		

Passenger List 1858-59

		Charles	8m		
Johnston		Samuel	45		Stone Mason
		Ellen	40		
		John	13		
		Ellen	9		
Jones		Robert	39		Shoemaker
		Hannah	33		
		Robert	14	Trans to single men.	
		Charles	11		
		John	6		
		Fredrick	3		
		Hannah	3m		
		Richard			Agricultural labourer
Joyce		Thomas	21		Labourer
		Anna	20		
		William	Infant		
Keetley		Henry	29		Farm Labourer
		Mary Ann	24		
Lambert		Isaac	32		
		Rebecca	29		
		Edward	7		
		William	5		
		Annie	2		
Lee		Samuel	24		Labourer
		Hester	21		
Lewis		Charles	28		Labourer

		Caroline	26		
		Phillipa Jane	2		
Lilley		Jonathan	32		Farm Labourer
		Maria	33		
		Reuben	10		
		Lucy	8		
		James	6		
		Geroge	5		
		Harry	3		
Lowe		Levi	37		Labourer
		Matilda	34		
		Eli	15	Trans to Singlemen	Shoemaker
		Mary Ann	12		
		Edward	8		
		Thomas	6		
		John	1		*Died at sea 01/12/1859*
Martin		Henry	32		Labourer
		Sarah	27		
		Sarah Ellen	3		
Martin		Philip	44		Bricklayer
		Mary	43		
		Elizabeth	6		
Milligan		Hugh	44		Labourer
		Margaret	42		
		Elizabeth	22	Trans to single women	Dressmaker

Passenger List 1858-59

		Huge	21	Trans to single men	Labourer
		James	19	Trans to single men	Labourer
		Sarah	17	Trans to single woman	Dressmaker
		Tom B	16	Trans to Single men	Sail maker
		Elizabeth	14		Dress maker
		William	11		
		Isaac	6		
		Margaret	4		
	Mills	George	9		
		John	8		
		Albert	5		
	Moody	John	31		Labourer
		Ann	33		
		Samual	10		
		Emma	8		
		Mary Ann	4		
	Newsome	Jeremiah	30		Tailor
		Hannah	28		
		William	7		
		Benjamin	5		
		Mary	3		
		Joseph	1		*Died at sea 02/01/1859*
	Nock	Richard	34		Bookbinder
		Sarah	33		
		Clara	5		

		Richard Henry	1		
Painter		Joseph	29		Carpenter
		Emma	28		
		Frederick	3		*Died at sea 29/12/1858*
Pawsey		John R.	31	Suffolk	Labourer
		Mary	39		
		John	13		
		Benjamin	11		
		George	8		
		Joseph	6		
		Martha	2		
Piper		William	45		Labourer
		Emma	45		
		Edward	21	Trans to single men	Labourer
		Jane	19	Trans to single women	Domestic servant
		Ellen	18	Trans to single women	Domestic servant
		Mary	15	Trans to single women	Domestic servant
		Henry	12		
		Martha	10		
		Alfred	7		
		Emma	5		
Power		William	23		Labourer
		Mary	25		
Pratt		James			

		Wife and child			
Purcell		William	29		Agricultural Labourer
		Bridget	27		
Rayers		William	37		Labourer
		Hannah	37		
Reeves		Thomas	37		Labourer
		Mary Ann	33		
		Thomas	12		
		Jane	11		
		George	9		
		Richard	6		
		William	2		
		Ruth	Infant Twin		
		Samuel	Infant Twin		
Robbins		George	27		Gardener
		Elizabeth	30		
		Emma	3		
		Elizabeth	1		
Rogers		William			
		Wife			
Saunders		Charles	31		Carpenter
		Hannah	32		
		Matilda	11		
Slater		Henry	40		Saywer & Labourer
		Ann	37		

		Mary Ann	19	Trans to Single women	
		Elizabeth	11		
Stephenson		William	35		Carpenter
		Elizabeth	39		
		George	1		
Stewart		Edward	30		Gardner & Weaver
		Elizabeth	33		
Tompkins		John	60		Tinplate Worker
		Elizabeth	59		
Toppin		Thomas			
		Wife			
Triggs		James	36		Farm Labourer
		Sarah	26		
		Robert	2		
Turner		Charles	35		Gardner & Brickmaker
		Mary Ann	33		
		Maria	11		
		Mary Ann	8		
		Jonah	6		
		Henry	4		
Watt		Alexander	53		Agricultural Labourer
		Sophia F			
		Agnes	21	Trans to Single Women	Domestic servant
		Sophia	19	Trans to Single Women	Domestic servant

Passenger List 1858-59

	Margaret	17	Trans to Single Women	Domestic servant
	John	15	Trans to Single men	Servant
	Isabella	13		Domestic Servant
	Mary	9		
	Eliza	6		
	Robina	4		
	Jessie	1		
Weastell	Anthony	41		Carpenter
	Jane	45		
	Marmaduke	16	Trans to Single Men	Carpenter
	George	14	Trans to Single men	Plumber
	John	7		
Weeber	Joseph	36		Labourer
	Eliza	38		
	Joseph	14		Labourer
	Fredrick	11		
	Mary Ann	8		
	John	6		
	Alfred	3		
Wilson	Mary	25		
	child	4		
Woodhead	George	46		Shepherd
	Harriet	47		
	Mary	19	Trans to Single Women	

Passenger List 1858-59

	Ellen	17	Trans to Single Women	
	John	15		
	George	13		
	Joseph	8		
Single Men	*Name*	*Age*	*Location*	*Occupation/Notes*
Aldrich	Edward	26		Labourer
Atkinson	John			
Atkinson	Henry			
Atkinson	Richard			
Ballantyne	James			
Bell	James			Servant
Billens	Frederick			
Buillens	Henry			
Cain	Hanse			
Cain	David			
Chapman	James			
Chapman	William			
Clark	Wm			
Collett	William (Ward of Sarah)	10		
Elmes	William			
Evans	Richard			Carpenter
Griffiths	John	29		Labourer
Horrell	George	26		Labourer
Johnston	John			
Jaggar	A. Hughes	25		Printer
Kibblewhite	Edward	18		Stockman

Kibblewhite	Henry	16		Carpenter
Jones	Robert	14		
Lee	Thomas	27		Clothmaker
Lewin	John J.	22		Wheelwright
Lewis	William	24		Farm Labourer
Lister	John	37		Shepherd
Lowe	Eli			
Mather	George			
Milligan	Hugh			
Milligan	James			
Milligan	Thomas			
Mallinder	James	24		Domestic Servant
Munro	Robert			
Nurse	Martin	30		Labourer
Pawsey	John R			
Philips	George		*Stow-way*	Cooper
Rowell	James	22		Labourer
Rawle	James	23		Agricultural Labourer
Piper	Edward			
Piper	Henry			
Reetz	Hubertus	27		
Reeves	James			
Skilling	John/James	21		Labourer
Stringer	Richard	22		Labourer
Swallow	Joshua	18		Brickmaker
Watt	John			

Weastell	Marmaduke			
Weastell	George			
Weeber	Joseph			
Wilder	Edward	20		Gardener
Woodhead	John			
Woodhead	George			
Single Women	*Name*	*Age*	*Location*	*Occupation/Notes*
Atkinson	Margaret			
Bell	Elizabeth			Domestic Servant
Callett	Sarah	52		
Cain	Mary			
Gapes	Esther			
Halstead	Louisa	21		Weaver
Jaggar	Susannah E.	21		School Mistress
Lowe	Mary Ann			
Martin	Emma	22		Domestic Servant
Martin	Mary Ann	18		Domestic Servant
Martin	Martha	13		
Martin	Sarah	25		Domestic Servant
Mulligan	Sarah			
Mulligan	Elizabeth			
Nurse	Catherine	18		Domestic Servant
Parrott	Catherine	26		Seamstress
Piper	Jane			
Piper	Ellen			

Passenger List 1858-59

Piper	Mary			
Slater	Mary Ann			
Robson	Alice	17		
Watt	Agnes			
Watt	Sophia			
Watt	Margaret			
Watt	Isabella			
Woodhead	Mary			
Woodhead	Ellen			

Passenger List 1859-60

Officers & Crew				
Name		**Duty**		
Barclay	A. W. Esq.	Capt		Part Owner of Ship
Stokes	18	Midshipman	*Died at sea 06/01/1860*	
Unknown	Mrs	Cook		
	Son		*Died at sea 10/01/1860*	
Stone		Doctor		
Chief Cabin Passengers	*Name*	*Age*	*Location*	*Occupation/Notes*
Bethell	Mr			
Duncan	Mr			
Erskine	Mr			
Fowler	Mr			
Howes	Mr			
Mellesh	Mr			
Povey	Miss			
Povey	Mr			
Rose	Mr			
Silk	Mr			
Simpson	Mr			
Soulsey	Mr			
	Mrs			
	Child			
Sproul	Mr			
Vachell	Mr			
Woodley	Miss			
White (Listed as Wright)	Mr	36	Suffolk	Died at sea - ***27/02/1860***
	Mrs			
2nd Cabin Passengers				
Ashton	Mr			
Aubin*	Mr			
Brown	Mr			
Elderton	Mr			
	Mrs			
	Child			
Hodge	Mr			

Passenger List 1859-60

McFlae*	Mr			
	Son	4		Died at sea - 31/12/1860
Perkins	Mr			
Plunket	Mr W	23		Died at sea - 29/01/1860
Thompson	Mr			
Wilson	Miss			
Paying Steerage Passengers	*Name*	*Age*	*Location*	*Occupation/Notes*
Bunting	William			
	Mrs			
Cook*	Mrs			
	Son	8		Died at sea - 13/02/1860
Driver	William			
	Andrew			
Fraser	Robert			
Foggarty	Julia			
Haig	Sidney			
	James			
Harbison	John			
Kirk	William			
Rayner	Mrs T			
	9 children (not named)			
Standon	Mr G			
	Mrs			
Warren*	Mr			
	Mrs			
	Child	5		Died at sea 06/01/1860
Assisted Passengers	**Families & Children**	*Age*	*Location*	*Occupation/Notes*
Aldridge	Thomas	30	Herts	Horse Keeper
	Ann	27		
Allen	John	41	Worcestershire	Gardener
	Emma	42		
	Thomas	10		
	Anne	6		
	Samuel	3		Died at sea - 26/12/1859
Armitage	Richard	48	Nottingham	Labourer
	Mary	48		

		William Henry	20	Trans to Single Men.	
		James	16	Trans to Single Men.	
		Samuel	7		
Ashman		George	40	Suffolk	Farm Labourer
		Jane	39		
		Mary Ann	18	Trans to Single Woman	
		Robert	17	Trans to Single Woman	
		Ellen	8		Died at sea - 4/02/186
Baldwin		Fielding	27	Yorkshire	Painter
		Martha	26		
		George sharp	6		
Begg		William	26	Forfarshire	Labourer
		Helen	28		
		Ann	3		
		Margaret	12 mths		*Died at sea - 13/02/1860*
Berry		James	31	Suffolk	Farm Labourer
		Susan	31		*Died at sea - 13/03/1860*
		Jane	12	Trans to Single Woman	
		Emma	10		
		Susannah	8		
		Caroline	7		
		George	5		
		Marianne	4		*Died at sea - 23/01/1860*
		Ellen	1		*Died at sea - 13/01/1860*
		Daughter			*Born on board 12/03/1860 Died at sea -13/03/1860*
Bevoy		*James*		*Suffolk*	*Not on passenger list but present on board.*
		Wife and 6 children			
Blomfield		Henry	31	Suffolk	Labourer
		Elizabeth	30		
		Henry	6		
		Ann	4		
		William	2		
		Ellen	10 months		*Died at sea - 01/02/186*
Burrows		William	29	Suffolk	

Passenger List 1859-60

	Susan	22			
	Ellen	Infant			
Burrows	George	32	Yorkshire	Miner	
	Caroline	29			
	Martha	7			
	Mary	5			
	Hannah	3			
	Thomas	2		*Died at sea - 13/01/1860*	
	George Clontarf			*Born at sea 16/01/1860* *Died a sea 03/02/1860*	
Bush	James	29	Middlesex	Painter	
	Sarah	21			
Butterfield	John	27	Yorkshire	Farm Labourer	
	Sarah	20			
Byron	Ralph	30	Middlesex	Carpenter	
	Rhoda	25			
Carey	George	35	Forfarshire	Farm Labourer	
	Crichton	32			
Carr	Henry	34	Yorkshire	Miner	
	Jane	33			
	Martha Ann	11			
	Catherine	9			
	Elizabeth	7			
	George Henry	2		*Died at sea - 19/02/1860*	
Carnock	Sophia	21	Middlesex	Husband on board as Steward	
Coatman	Joseph	45	Cambridgeshire	Roadmaker	
	Mary	50			
	Joseph	12	Trans to Single Men.		
	Betsey	5			
	Eliza	2			
	Charlotte (absent.)	Infant		*Presumed died just before boarding.*	
Day	William	25	Hertfordshire	Gardener	
	Grace	27			
Dearnaley	Edwin	31	Cheshire	Carpenter	
	Sarah	28			
Double	Robert	25	Suffolk		
	Harriet	22			

		Ann	6 weeks old		
Early		Samuel	45	Hants	Carpenter
		Elizabeth	42	Trans to Single Woman	
		Eliza	20	Trans to Single Woman	
		Stephen	19	Trans to Single Woman	
		Elizabeth	17		
		Samuel	15		
		George	13		
		Ellen sarah	11		
		William	9		
		Charles	7		
		Frederic	3		
		Mary Louise	6 mth		
Faires		Thomas Jackson	48	Colchester	Saddler
		Janet	40		
		James	16	Trans to Single Men.	
		Robert	14	Trans to Single Men.	
		Thomas	11		
		Marion	9		
		Janet	7		
		George	5		
		Lucy Emma	18 months		*Died at sea - 31/12/1859*
Frame		James	48	Lanarkshire	Ploughman
		Janet	40		
		James	16		
		Robert	14		
		Thomas	11		
		Marion	9		
		Janet	7		
		George	5		
Friers		Thomas	George		Saddler
		Sarah	26		
		Lucy Emma	1		
Greengoe		William	29	Sussex	Farm Labourer

Passenger List 1859-60

		Elizabeth	26		
		Mary Ann	2		
Galletly		Alexander	58	*Perth* Trans to Single Men.	Farm Labourer
		Alexander jr.	24	Trans to Single Men.	Ploughman
		John	18		Ploughman
		James	15	Trans to Single Men.	Ploughman
		Andrew	13	Trans to Single Men.	
		Barbara	11	Trans to Single Woman	
		Margaret	9	Trans to Single Woman	
Hargood		James	38	Surrey	Gardener
		Sarah	35		
		Alfred John	21	Trans to Single Men	Gardener
		William	16	Trans to Single Woman	
		James	12	Trans to Single Men	
		Sarah	10		
		Robert	6		*Died at sea - 03/01/1860*
		Charlotte	4		*Died at sea - 25/02/1860*
		Francis	8 mths		
Glover		Helena	15	Trans to Single Woman	NIECE TO HARGOOD'S family
Hawthorne		Joseph	30	Worcestershire	Shoemaker
		Alice	26		
		Maria	12		
		Emma	11		
		Louisa Alice	4		
		Maria	1		*Died at sea - 15/01/1860*
		Son			*Born at sea – died 11/03/1860*
Jones		Thomas	28	Stafford	Labourer
		Hannah	29		
		William	1		

Passenger List 1859-60

		Thomas	3 mths		
Jones		Abraham	38	Suffolk	Farm Labourer
		Rebekah	35		
		Walter	16	Trans to Single Men.	
		Marianne	13	Trans to Single Woman	
		Susan	11		
		Emma	8		
		Arthur	5		
		Charles	3		*Died at sea - 28/12/1859*
		Charlotte	Infant		
Judson		William	30	Leicester	Labourer
		Sarah	30		
		James	12	Trans to Single Men.	
		Elizabeth	10		
		Laybell	7		
		Sarah Ann	3		
		Martha	4 mths		*Died at sea - 13/01/1860*
Kane		Patrick	29	Derbyshire	Farm Labourer
		Bridget	26		
		Rosamund	1		
Knapp		George	25	Leicester	Farm Labourer
		Mary	21		
		Elizabeth	2		
Lord		Jabez	22	Yorkshire	Blacksmith
		Mary	22		
McCarthy		Michael	28	Queens Co.	Ploughman
		Julia	26		
		Maria	3		
McGosker		John	26	Durham	Mason
		Mabella	26		
McLauchlan		James	25		
		Ann	27		
		James	2 months		
Mitton		Walter	27		
		Mary Ann	27		
		Mary Ann	8		
		Sarah	5		

		William	2		*Died at sea - 30/12/1859*
		Emily	11 m		*Died at sea - 15/01/1860*
Parker		James Smith	35	Surrey	Mechanic
		Sarah	32		
		John	8		
		James	5		
		Mary Ann	2		
		Elizabeth	6 m		*Died at sea - 23/12/1859*
Patterson		Thomas	30	Perth	Labourer
		Elizabeth	32		
Preston		Henry	26	Lancashire	Labourer
		Ann	26		
		Thomas William	6		
		James	2		
		Sarah Jane	7 weeks		
Ritchie		Andrew	40	Forfarshire	
		Susan	40		
		David	12	Trans to Single Men.	
		George	11		
		Alexander	7		
		Andrew	5		
		James	3		*Died at sea - 29/12/1859*
Rouse		James	39	Suffolk	Groom
		Maria	37		
		James	17	Trans to Single Men.	
		Maria	16	Trans to Single Woman	
		Charles	14	Trans to Single Men.	
		Walter	13	Trans to Single Men.	
		Alfred	10		
		Thomas	9		
		Henry (Recorded incorrectly as Mary)	7		*Died at sea - 18/02/1860*
		Benjamin	2		
Ryan		Patrick	29	Tipperary	Labourer

		Anna	29		
Sadler		Thomas	24	Suffolk	Groom
		Sarah	25		
		Harry	4		
		Betsey	3		*Died at sea - 13/01/1860*
		Thomas	11m		*Died at sea - 11/01/1860*
Seager		Henry Fowle	36	Middlesex	Compositer
		Charlotte	31		
		Henry Fowle	6		
		Charlotte Elizabeth	2		
		Amy Eliza	2		*Died at sea - 03/02/1860*
		Annie	2 months		
Seaward		Emmanuel	23	Dorset	Labourer
		Ann	26		
Sheeham		Martin	43	Kings Co.	Farm Labourer
		Bridget	35		
		John	10		
		Kate	5		
		Mary	11 m		
Smart		Thomas	25	Armagh	Farm Labourer
		Sarah	25		
Smart		Archibald	28	Armagh	Farm Labourer
		Anne	29		
		John	8		
		Anne	5		
		Martha	3		
		Ralpth	Infant		
Turner		Joseph	44	Stafford	Carpenter
		Ann	48		
		John	14	Trans to Single Men.	
		Sarah ann	12	Trans to Single Woman	
Waller		William (*Escorting family*)		Edinburgh	Employed on board
		Jane	26		
		Robert James	5		*Died at sea - 11/01/1860*
		Edward Corrgill	3		
		Benjamin Bruce	12 m		*Died at sea - 23/12/1859*

Walters	Rees William	34		Stafford	Carpenter
	Sarah	38			
	Rees Jones	6			
	George John	12 m			Died at sea - 17/01/1860
Wilkinson	Robinson	30		Lincolnshire	Blacksmith
	Harriet	24			
	Elizabeth	6			Died at sea - 08/01/1860
	Hannah	3			
Williams	Richard	28		Kent	
	Barbara	26			
	Edgar George	4			
	Barbara	2			
	Barbara	2			
	Edward Richard	6 months			
Wright	Robert	32		Suffolk	Labourer
	Harriet	28			
	Edward	12		Trans to Single Men.	
	Pamela	9			
	Arthur	5			
	Amelia	11m			Died at sea - 07/01/1860
	Son				Born on board - 05/02/1860 Died on board - 13/03/1860
Single Men	*Name*	*Age*		*Location*	*Occupation/Notes*
Armitage	William Henry	20		Nottingham	Labourer
	James	16		Nottingham	Labourer
Ashman	Robert	17		Suffolk	Labourer
Beardsmore	William	26		Nottingham	Carpenter
Blomfield	Mark			Suffolk	Labourer
Briggs	Thomas	28		Yorkshire	Farm Labourer
Canneen	Patrick	27		Clare	Farm Labourer
Cook	Archibald	23		Aryshire	Joiner
Coatman	Joseph	12		Cambridgeshire	Labourer
Dallas	George	30		Kings Co.	Soldier
Early	Stephen	19		Hants	Carpenter
	Samuel	15		Hants	Labourer
	George	13		Hants	Labourer
Frame	James	16		Lanarkshire	Farm Labourer
Frame	Robert	14		Lanarkshire	Farm Labourer

Galletly	Alexander	58		Perth	Weaver
	Alexander	24		Perth	Ploughman
	John	18		Perth	Ploughman
	James	15		Perth	Ploughman
	Andrew	13			
Gibbs	James	26		Bedfordshire	Smith
Glover	Hawley	23		Leicester	Farm Labourer
	William	16		Surrey	Labourer
	James	12		Surrey	Labourer
Hargood	Alfred John	21		Surrey	Gardener
Jones	Walter	16		Suffolk	Farm Labourer
Judson	James	12		Leicester	Labourer
McConnachie	James	22		Banff	Labourer
McGuire	Norman	18		Kent	Labourer
Pey	Patrick	22		Kings Co.	Farm Labourer
Pope	John (son of Mary Coatman)	20		Stafford	Osler
Proctor	John	24		Stafford	Farm Labourer
Ritchie	David	12		Forfar	Labourer
Robertson	John	21		Banff	Farm Labourer
Rouse	James	17		Suffolk	Labourer
	Charles	14		Suffolk	Labourer
	Walter	13		Suffolk	Labourer
Smart	John	58		Armagh	Farm Labourer
	David	16		Armagh	Farm Labourer
	John Jnr	20		Armagh	Farm Labourer
Swannick	Samuel				Ship Schoolmaster
Turner	John	14		Stafford	Labourer
Watson	John	23		Wiltshire	Farm Labourer
Wright	Edward	12		Suffolk	Labourer
Single Women	*Name*	*Age*		*Location*	*Occupation/Notes*
Ashman	Mary Ann	18		Suffolk	Domestic Servant
Barton	Eliza (sister to Sarah Sadler)	18		Suffolk	Maid - *Died at sea - 07/02/1860*
Beardsmore	Jane	17		Nottingham	Milliner
Berry	Jane	12		Suffolk	Domestic Servant
Canneen	Anne	16		Clare	Domestic Servant
Carr	Elizabeth	42		Suffolk	Domestic Servant
Curd	Curtis Sarah	38			Ship Matron

Passenger List 1859-60

Denley	Jane	27	Nottinghamshire	Domestic Servant
Early	Eliza Jane	20	Hants	Domestic Servant
	Elizabeth	17	Hants	Domestic Servant
Galletly	Barbara	11	Perth	Domestic Servant
	Margaret	9	Perth	Domestic Servant
Glover	Helena	15	Surrey	Domestic Servant
Grimes	Sarah Ann	23	Surrey	Laundress
Hawthorne	Mira	12	Worcestershire	Domestic Servant
Jones	Marianne	13	Suffolk	Domestic Servant
McLeod	Jane	30	Middlesex	Laundress
	Donald	2		
Melville	Mary Ann	18	Forfar	Domestic Servant
Poore	Elizabeth	29	Bath	Housekeeper
Plant	Mary	19	Yorkshire	Domestic Servant
Pope	Jemima (Nina) (Daughter of Mary Coatman)	18	Cambridge	Domestic Servant
Proctor	Jane Ann	22	Staffordshire	Dairy Maid
Reynolds	Eliza	28	Middlesex	Domestic Servant
Rouse	Maria	16	Suffolk	Domestic Servant
Smart	Mary Ann	18	Armagh	Domestic Servant
Turner	Sarah Ann	12	Staffordshire	Domestic Servant
Westwood	Emma	26	Warwick	Domestic Servant
Wilson	Elizabeth	37	Staffordshire	Milliner

Bibliography

Primary Sources

Accounts and papers of the House of Commons – Shipping. Sessions 1867-1868 vol LXIII. Section relating to the sinking of *Clontarf*, 1868.

Acland, John Barton Arundel, *Diary 1858 – 60.* c.1860. Transcribed by Hearnshaw, V. and Blakeley, K. University of Canterbury, 1994.

Acland, John Barton Arundel, *Shipping papers 'Clontarf, A1': ships regulations and plan, Sep. 1855.*

University of Canterbury, 1994.

Early, Stephen, *Ship-Board Dairy 1859-60.* Wellington Archives

Perkins, William - *Log Of A Voyage From London to New Zealand (Otago Settlers Museum)*

Passenger List, Clontarf voyage 1859-60 (in original and text form), Christchurch Library Archives.

Passenger List, Clontarf voyage 1859-60. Transcribed by Corey Woodward, courtesy of yesteryears.co.nz, 2011

Passenger List, Clontarf voyage 1859-60. Archives New Zealand IMCH4/29

Newspapers

Lyttelton Times (Canterbury)

The Press (Canterbury)

The Star (Canterbury)

London Standard (UK)

Secondary sources

Duncan, Alfred H. *Early Days in New Zealand.* London: Simpkin, Marshall, & Co., 1888.

Migrant Ships of the 19th Century. NZ Maritime News vol. 38, 1980.

Early Settlement of Canterbury. Christchurch: Canterbury Times, 1892

Weeks, Horace J. *The Cyclopaedia of New Zealand [Canterbury Provincial District].* (Biographies of passengers 1858 -59), Christchurch, 1903.

White Wings *Vol. 1 Fifty Years of Sail In New Zealand Trade, 1850 to 1900.* Auckland: Brett Printing Co., 1924.

Image Sources

Backhouse, Edward. *Comet Donati as seen from Hexham*. 1858. Monochrome watercolour.

Butterfield, Lindsay. *Butterfield Family Photo*. (©Lindsay Butterfield, 2011. All rights reserved.)

Darling, David. *Encyclopedia of Science - Comets- Donati's Comet (C/1858 L1)*

Haast family. *Portrait of Edward Sealy*. Photographs (PA-Group-00377)

Illustrated Australian News. *Landing Immigrants at Lyttelton NZ , 23 January 1878*.

Illustrated London Press. *Misc illustrations - 1850 -1900*.

Illustrated NZ Herald. *Montage of Life on Board Emigrant Ship 1875*, 9 April 1875

Marriott ,Wayne P . *Lucy Brake, page 37*(© Wayne P Marriott 2011. All rights reserved.)

Solem, Borge. *Crew of a German Ship 1894* - © 2002.

Spurling, Jack. *Painting of the La Hogue*. From Lubbock, Basil. *SAIL: The Romance of the Clipper Ships*. London : Blue Peter Publishing 1927.

Websites

Historical Currency Conversions. Courtesy of National Archives, United Kingdom. nationalarchives.gov.uk/currency/

Papers Past. Digitised newspapers database courtesy of the National Library of New Zealand. paperspast.natlib.govt.nz

RootsWeb. *Clontarf shipping lists 1858-60*.

RootsWeb. *Margaret lyne - Waller family*

www.britishnewspaperarchive.co.uk

www.rootsweb.ancestry.com

www.ingramcontent.com/pod-product-compliance
Lightning Source LLC
Chambersburg PA
CBHW060419090426
42734CB00011B/2373